# The A-Z of popular scooters & microcars

## Cruising in style!

Michael Dan

**VELOCE PUBLISHING**
THE PUBLISHER OF FINE AUTOMOTIVE BOOKS

## Other great Veloce books –

# www.veloce.co.uk

First published in February 2007 by Veloce Publishing Limited, 33 Trinity Street, Dorchester DT1 1TT, England. Fax 01305 268864/e-mail info@veloce.co.uk/web www.veloce.co.uk or www.velocebooks.com
ISBN 13: 978 1 84584 088 4. UPC: 6-36847-04088.
Readers with ideas for automotive books, or books on other transport or related hobby subjects, are invited to write to the editorial director of Veloce Publishing at the above address.
British Library Cataloguing in Publication Data - A catalogue record for this book is available from the British Library. Typesetting, design and page make-up all by Veloce Publishing Ltd on Apple Mac.
Printed in India by Replika Press.

Page design and layout by Jude Brooks.

# Contents

# What the book sets out to do

My book is an attempt to recreate the scene and atmosphere of 1950s Britain when scooters and microcars first had a significant impact upon our streets and, for the first time, my generation was able to afford convenient personal transport which also had a bright new style and image. I hope, also, that it provides the data and detail necessary to serve as a reference source, together with many happy recollections of that era.

New cars were beyond the pocket of most, and those who could afford one had to wait many months for delivery. After the Second World War most new cars were exported in order to bring badly needed money into the UK. The second-hand car market was small and those cars that were available were of less sophisticated design. Streets were not lined with parked cars as they are today. Unless you were happy to dress up in heavy motorcycle clothing the only economic forms of transport were bus, coach or a steam train, and it certainly was not usual to have your own private transport.

At that time, most photography was in black and white; colour photographs were expensive and rare, as was colour advertising in magazines. As the general economic situation improved, colour advertising grew more prolific at around the time the first scooters and microcars put in an appearance. Hire purchase – a cash deposit and monthly payment scheme – meant that personal transport became a possibility for many and public response to this

meant a rapid increase in sales of these two easier to afford forms of transport. The vehicles could be made in much smaller factories by fewer people than conventional cars, and were thus cheaper and easier to produce. Their affordability and fresh, new style made them popular with all age groups.

The Italian Vespa was the first scooter to be seen on British roads in the early 1950s. This was a very important machine which formed the basis for the regeneration of that country's decimated industry after the war. Lambretta scooters – another success story – followed, and were distributed all around the world with many countries eventually producing them under licence alongside their own makes and models.

Sales of conventional motorcycles began to drop and soon magazines dedicated to this new form of transport appeared on newsstands, taking sales from the rather drab weekly motorcycle publications. *Scooter World* first appeared in 1956 and, with its bright yellow cover, championed the cause of all things scooter, often replying to criticism published in motorcycle magazines claiming that scooters were both unsafe and unpatriotic. *Scooter and Threewheeler* magazine followed, initially with dull green cover as per the established motorcycle magazines but later changed to the same bright yellow as *Scooter World, which* came to signify the sunshine world of scootering.

Microcars also grew in popularity at around the same time, primarily in the UK, France and Germany. There was an immediate demand for a small,

*Members of the Bristol scooter club assemble for a run in 1960, with a couple of microcars thrown in for good measure.*

affordable covered vehicle. Germany also found that these vehicles were a sound basis on which to regenerate its industry, helping to rebuild the fortunes of companies such as BMW and, later, Audi. (This explains why there are many German museums featuring scooters and microcars.)

Scooter clubs were formed by enthusiasts and it became a common sight to see club runs at weekends on Britain's roads, lines of scooters with male and female riders in convoy out into the country, or off to the coast. There would often be a dozen colourful scooters with a row of microcars bringing up the rear, all proudly bearing club banners and pennants.

The natural progression from scooters was microcars as they used similar air-cooled engines, were advertised in the same magazines, cost only a little more to run and maintain, could be driven on the same driving licence, and were sold by the same dealers. Purchase price then was much less than that of a conventional car, and their designs and bright appearance set them apart from other vehicles.

Scooters and microcars, and the owner's clubs associated with them, expanded the horizons of so many people, young and old alike. Not only were they an affordable means of transport for the necessities of life, such as getting to work or going shopping, they also made travelling out of the towns and cities and into the countryside affordable. Manufacturers' advertising made much of this fact, often featuring their machines in interesting scenic backgrounds with happy, carefree riders. Contemporary advertising had a fascinating period style which not only demonstrated the appeal of these new vehicles, but also gave an insight to the sort of people who purchased them and how they enjoyed using them.

Production of conventional cars improved in time and purchase prices became more affordable. As a result, scooter and microcar sales initially took a downturn, then, as new purchasers opted instead for the greater comfort and convenience of the modern car, their markets declined and they eventually virtually disappeared. Only a few enthusiasts kept some of the more popular makes of scooter on the streets, whilst microcars more or less vanished from everyday traffic.

The scooter and microcar experience – life-changing for many, and certainly for me! – is one of affordable style, innovation, colour and convenience; the sharing of a common bond between like-minded people with the same interests; amazement and sorrow at the decline, coupled with nostalgia for a different world, long gone. In later years, the experience was embodied in pride in conservation and restoration, and scooter and microcar rebirth into the modern market.

In the last twenty or so years there has been a rapid growth in the restoration of classic scooters and microcars, as so many people have fond memories of the machines that transformed their lives back in the late 1950s and early 1960s. People who – teenagers then – now have grown up families, and more money and time to spend on restoring their beloved vehicles.

Shown in the first photo overleaf is a display stand of the Vintage Motor Scooter Club (VMSC) at the Stafford Classic Bike Show. This is the main UK club for all those interested in learning about the history, restoration and running of all makes of scooter, including Vespa and Lambretta. There is especial support in the club for all the more unusual makes: the rarer the machine the more reward there is, and praise from fellow members, in eventually seeing it back on the road in original running order! Shown on display on this occasion are restored scooters from the UK, Germany and the USA. Members, however, own machines from as far afield as Poland, Russia, South America and New Zealand.

The second photo (below) was taken at a National Microcar Rally which, incidentally, also always welcomes scooters. Generally speaking, the restoration of microcars is more expensive and difficult to complete. Very often vehicles are imported in an incomplete state and worked on in order to eventually have something unique. Today, it is possible to see restored microcars that were never UK imports in the 1950s or 1960s. Modern microcars are also seen at "the National" as they are still relatively rare. The rally often has a range of vehicles which are not true microcars but whose owners feel an affinity with microcars; as such, they are interesting and very welcome.

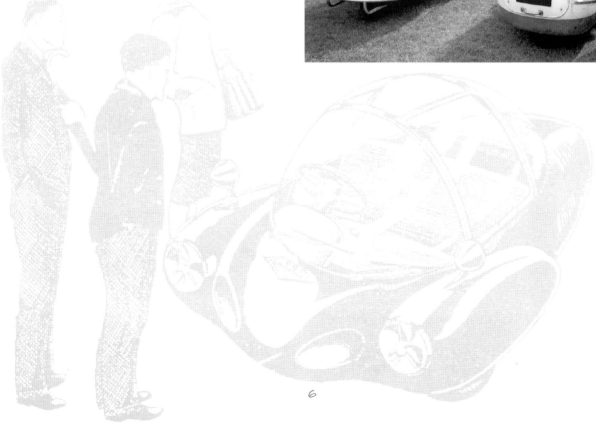

# Introduction

As you may have probably already guessed, scooters and microcars have been a lifelong passion for me. I hope you will excuse the inclusion of some personal experiences, which very many people – searching for economic personal transport – shared back in the 1950s and 1960s. In today's world many thousands of enthusiasts are actively involved in the restoration of these classic machines; many more visit indoor and outdoor shows to see them, and are quite often surprised that so many makes and models were available.

Scooters were a very significant part of life for me as a teenager growing up in the UK in the 1950s. They were the only form of personal transport I could afford and, luckily, were my preferred choice as they stood out from the crowd, were convenient, and a breath of fresh air compared to the drab prewar designs of motorcycles and cars seen on the road at the time.

My first motorised vehicle was a scooter; a new type of vehicle which I truly believed was superior to the oily and dirty motorcycles I had come across. I had left home to start my first job over a hundred miles away, and needed cheap personal transport to get to and from work and visit home and my parents. I chose a British-made Piatti, bought for me by my parents when I was seventeen (the older generation

Going my way? A Cyclemaster Piatti with a period bus on Plymouth Hoe.

still had significant reservations about buying anything foreign-made), and imports were subject to an extra tax imposed by the government.

The Piatti was made in Surrey by an established company well known for making the Cyclemaster powered rear bicycle wheel, another transport revolution which would fit a normal bicycle that had become quite popular and widespread as it took the hard work out of cycling. The Piatti scooter offered a sleek body on a bright, colourful-looking machine, and was cheaper to buy than the more popular and widely-seen Italian Vespa and Lambretta.

It is hard to fully appreciate today what a significant difference scooters made to personal transport at that time. They were affordable to buy, economic to run, and becoming popular everywhere. They had style, kept you relatively clean and dry via built-in legshields and footboards (most owners opted for the large windscreen styled to suit a particular scooter as additional weather protection), and seemed to instil a special pride in ownership as their riders were set apart from the crowds waiting for a bus, or heavily dressed in protective clothing on a conventional motorcycle.

Today, of course, personal transport is taken for granted but, back then, the usual way that folk got around was by bus, coach – or steam train! It also took longer to get anywhere due to much narrower roads. Most people could not afford a car, and those that could had to endure long waiting lists at dealers. The second-hand car market was very small and so scooters offered an attractive modern alternative, together with a new area of social life in the form of clubs where owners could get together and socialise, and also take part in organised club runs to the countryside and coast. This, in itself, was something new to be enjoyed.

My Piatti was replaced a year or so later by another British-made scooter, the DKR Defiant. This was chosen for me by my parents, who were again paying for it. They considered my choice of a German Maicoletta to be unpatriotic and expensive, and besides, how would it be possible to obtain spares from Germany? Although the 200cc DKR was okay (it did have the luxury of an electric starter), it was easily out-performed by 150cc Vespas and Lambrettas. Neither the Piatti nor the DKR was really suitable for the long-distance travelling I was subjecting them to, in any case, which I learned from experience!

Eventually, I was able to afford to buy a replacement myself: a second-hand Dayton Albatross, another British machine but purchased on merit rather than patriotism! This was a fine machine which I kept for fourteen years, and it gave me my best and most rewarding years on two wheels.

In the fifties a motorcycle licence allowed the holder to drive both a scooter and a microcar, provided the microcar's reverse gear had been disabled. This was simply done either by fitting a plate to restrict the movement of the gearstick, or by fitting an electrical switch to disconnect the reverse contact breakers. There was no need for the expense or inconvenience of taking another driving test, so it was a natural progression to upgrade from one means of transport to the other when the time came to purchase a vehicle that could offer more space,

comfort and weather protection. Microcars were also much cheaper to buy than second-hand conventional cars, which were still in short supply, and would cover many more miles to the gallon than could regular cars.

Most microcars employed air-cooled, small capacity engines that were similar to those used in scooters. For my first microcar I chose a Messerschmitt bubblecar, primarily because of its individual style and narrow width, living up to its name of Cabin Scooter. The engine was the same as that fitted in the Prior Viscount scooter. A friend had one of these fine German machines and it impressed me with its performance, reliability and economy. It was possible to take a full driving test in a microcar which would then allow the use of reverse gear, which is what I later did. Many years later it felt most odd to drive a normal, full-sized car whilst sitting on one side of the vehicle (in the Messerschmitt the occupants sit one behind the other in the centre of the car).

Scooters and microcars continued to grow in popularity all over the world well into the 1960s, when sales fell off quite dramatically in most western countries because of increased family income and falling prices of conventional motorcars.

In the late eighties I returned to these individual machines when I became involved in the restoration of classic transport as a hobby. Very few people were restoring scooters from the fifties, as this was well before the second boom in scooter sales when the very name 'scooter' was in danger of being consigned to the past. On the road then were the petite, small-engined Japanese runabouts, which became known as 'mopeds', a name which really applied to an earlier form of motorised bicycle.

During the nineties I was able to find, restore and maintain a series of these fascinating classic microcars. First was a Heinkel bubblecar, followed by a Messerschmitt, a labour of love in rememberance of a fine machine that gave me many happy memories. Later, I again became involved with scooters, starting with a Maicoletta from Germany, a machine I had long wanted as a teenager, but which my parents could not be persuaded to pay for.

As I restored various scooters I spent time researching their history. Club magazines published articles I wrote as a result, and it was suggested that these should be properly recorded in a more permanent form, hence the idea of this book.

Photographing all sorts of scooters over the

years has also been an interest of mine and included are pictures of those models I have seen, together with those which have passed through my hands for restoration. I thought I would present some of these photos in a more unusual and relevant way. Consequently, besides conventional shots, thanks to computer wizardry, some images show the vehicles in more interesting places, or with a range of other classic vehicles of the same period.

A Vespa Rod model parked alongside Bristol buses of the 1950s.

Those models I personally restored were a small proportion of the range that was available in the Good Old Days! Enthusiasts from all over the UK – and abroad – have been able to find and restore many more, including some rare machines. Included in this book are photographs I have taken of well over two hundred different scooters and microcars restored by other enthusiasts. It is great that there are people who are interested enough to involve themselves in this restoration work. Take a look at these fine machines and enjoy the variety and design variations offered by the great range of companies which produced motor scooters and microcars in the fifties and sixties. Marvel at the restorations that give the impression of the machines being new and untouched, straight from the factory, whereas, in fact, very often they started out as incomplete and rusting wrecks that most people would have left for scrap. A lot of time, money, skill and effort has gone into the restoration of these unique and classic vehicles.

We are fortunate that, today, interest is strong, to the extent that even many diverse makes and models have been restored. There are still gaps in what was available and, as time goes by, it becomes more difficult to find them and the parts required for their restoration. However, in this book, you can see machines that were rare even way back when!

The fifties and sixties were unique periods in the history of the motor scooter, microcar and personal transport in general. On today's roads, we see again a new range of these machines, still offering economy, convenience and style.

I hope my book will serve as a reminder to all of us who remember, used to use and still love these machines. We were pioneers of a new form of transport which almost nearly died out in the 1970s, yet set the trend for the future.

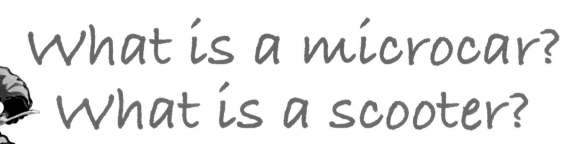

# What is a microcar? What is a scooter?

A microcar is essentially just a little car! Matters can be a little more precise, such as specifying certain engine capacity limits, maximum body sizes, number of seats, etc, but here there are exceptions to the rules and things can get a little complicated. A microcar is designed primarily as an economy vehicle, perhaps smaller physically and in engine capacity to the more conventional car in its quest to be more economic to purchase and run.

At the heart of these 1950s vehicles are the so-called bubblecars from Germany, and the British-designed, small economy cars that were originally called minicars. At microcar rallies you can see examples of cars that perhaps aren't particularly economic or very small either, but are different in design to run-of-the-mill vehicles. If their owners feel they have an affinity with microcars then these vehicles are of interest and welcome; they've certainly been included in this book.

Such is the interest worldwide for unusual vehicles that, today, you can see examples of British microcars on show in Austria and Australian microcars in France! In Canada many rare German microcars are displayed, some of which can no longer be seen in Germany. Many foreign microcars have been imported into the UK for restoration. In other countries the variety of vehicles which turn up at microcar rallies can be vast; very often, because a vehicle is rarely seen in that country this makes it special and worthy of inclusion as long as it isn't too large! In the USA, for example, 1960 Ford Anglias, Austin A35s and two-stroke Saabs – never seen at a British microcar rally – appear alongside the bubblecars. The term 'Mini' has been used in North America to designate these somewhat larger cars probably because, originally, the name of the Morris Mini was little known there and, compared to most home-grown American cars, they *are* small.

A Scooter is a two-wheeled motorcycle which puts the comfort and convenience of the rider before its own basic mechanical requirements. For example, a motorcycle has a cross member for maximum rigidity, whereas on a scooter this area is open; a motorcycle uses relatively large, solid spoked rim wheels compared to a scooter's smaller disc wheels with split rims for easy puncture repair (plus, a scooter can carry a spare at the rear); a scooter is more comfortable to ride with its flat footboard rather than the tubular foot pegs on a motorcycle. Economy again comes into the equation, as does an engine with modest capacity, although there are exceptions to the rule. A stylish appearance and user-friendly appeal are prominent features. If it's not necessary to wear special clothing as protection against the weather or the machine's own mechanics, then it is most likely to be defined and accepted as a scooter. As the years have gone by, modern scooters with larger engines have become common and accepted.

In spite of the older machines generally having small engines, many owners delight in riding them on long journeys, perhaps as a test to use them in a

*Smile, please. A Heinkel Cabin Cruiser at a rally in Ashton Court, Bristol.*

way the designer never intended, and to prove to all that they and their vehicles can do it! In the 1950s and '60s this was also a way to generate publicity for scooters and microcars, and to demonstrate the economy possible on long journeys. There were many examples of scooters and microcars travelling where you wouldn't expect them to, such as across deserts, to the top of mountains and across continents. A scooter even crossed the English Channel with the help of floats and a propeller connected to the rear wheel!

Owners clubs were a large part of the scene then and organised events ranging from local meetings to large international rallies, which were attended by thousands of owners from all over the world. Famous personalities were often willing to present prizes at these events, and be associated with the attraction and appeal of scooters and microcars.

# The market place

The range of companies selling motor scooters on the British market has varied greatly in my lifetime. I first became aware of scooters as a teenager in the 1950s, up to which point, if you wanted the economy of two-wheeled transport, the only option was a motorcycle, which I considered a rather primitive device. Cars had moved on to offer weather protection and disc wheels long ago, but motorcycles still used spokes like a pedal cycle – and you had to ride them like a mechanical version of the horse! They weren't at all user-friendly, despite a few British attempts to civilise the motorcycle with the Gadabout and the Corgi, but even these were not very plentiful on the roads. They were still dull to look at and still made a lot of noise without offering much in the way of performance.

When the Vespa appeared on the scene its style and relatively quiet and efficient engine meant it stood out from the crowd. The user-friendly bodywork made it attractive and, although there wasn't a great range of colours first of all, it was a great improvement on the usually black motorcycles available. Soon, the Lambretta LD drew attention, too, and competition between these two Italian companies resulted in further improvement.

Then Germany came up with the NSU Prima D – which seemed an improvement on the Lambretta – and the Durkopp Diana, a fresh and more upmarket idea of what a scooter should offer and look like.

The Zundapp Bella and the Heinkel joined them, and soon it was possible to purchase scooters like the magnificent Maicoletta with extra performance. British makes such as the Dayton Albatross and Piatti Cyclemaster put in an appearance, even though Britain was late getting into scooter production. Soon, a very much larger range of models emerged from all sorts of European countries, and scooters became accepted and were a very familiar sight on our roads. France, Austria, Holland and Belgium were offering machines for sale in the UK, and these were welcomed for their merit.

The late 1950s and early 1960s became the peak years for productivity with a truly fabulous variety of available scooters. At this time, Britain manufactured a large range of respected motorcycles. BSA, one of the biggest British motorcycle manufacturers, was amongst the first to accept the challenge by developing the Beeza scooter, advertising it and showing a prototype at the National Earls Court Motorcycle Show. The company then had second thoughts and decided not to produce it for sale, which prompted other British motorcycle manufacturers to also hold back from scooter production. (The design was based on a sidevalve engine, which was well behind the times.) This was an early sign that the British motorcycle industry was beginning to lose its way, and the start of its decline.

Eventually, the UK got around to offering a respectable range of generally moderate scooter designs, mainly from much smaller companies not well known for their past involvement with motorcycle production. The big names in motorcycling did eventually follow suit when they saw the sales figures being achieved by these smaller companies. However, even when they produced designs that seemed to develop the scooter concept, somehow British manufacturers were unable to make a commercial success out of the venture; a great pity as some really excellent designs – featured in current magazine articles – never even made it into production, in spite of favourable reviews.

At this time many firms set up as importers to bring foreign machines into Britain. This was resisted by a relatively large percentage of the buying public as the idea that 'British is best' was still believed by many; anything foreign must, by its very nature, be cheap and second class. The government levied extra taxes on anything imported, and it was still considered unpatriotic to buy foreign-made goods. Scooters and bubblecars went a long way toward shaking up these stick-in-the-mud ideas as the younger generation saw and liked the vehicles straight away, displaying a much greater acceptance of them.

Italy was the biggest producer of scooters, which were selling in large numbers. Production in 1961 was nearly 500,000 scooters, five times greater than motorcycles. Germany came second with 70,000 scooters, followed by France with nearly 40,000; even Britain did well with 30,000. Conventional British motorcycles were still ruling the world with production figures of 130,000 machines. But compare that figure with European scooter production and it is obvious that scooters were the bikes of the future, or so we enthusiasts thought!

In the UK microcar market British designs were amongst the first and very successful. The only other foreign maker of microcars sold in Britain was West Germany, whose scooter products had already met with a high degree of acceptance amongst British buyers. Known as Cabin Scooters in their home country, 'bubblecar' was the collective term used in Britain. In fact, in the UK then the modern word microcar was not used at all. Most of the vehicles on offer were three-wheelers so were generally known as just that, though the term 'tricar' was sometimes used to describe them. Other nomenclature included 'economy' cars; 'lightweights'; 'midget' cars or dwarf cars. Miniature car or minicar were names generally used for small three- and four-wheeled economy cars. The diminutive Fiat 500 was accepted within

the miniature car grouping but, with the arrival of the Morris Mini in 1959, some confusion arose over the use of that name, as the Mini had much livelier performance and seemed more at home grouped with the conventional motorcar. The Austin clone of the Mini was initially called the Austin Seven, whilst the full name of the Morris was Mini Minor. The general public preferred and used the shorter Mini name and, eventually, this is what it became known as. Possibly, this was the reason why the term microcar gradually came to be used to indicate that these vehicles were even smaller than the Mini (even though, for many of them, this was only the case in engine capacity!). Alec Issigonis, British designer of the Mini, stated his intention to clear the streets of the imported bubblecars and, within a very few years, had virtually succeeded in this aim.

Long before the Mini there were British microcars: the Astra, the Atom, the RNW, the Sterling, the Rodley and the Russon, and even an interesting prototype 700cc car from Rover. Although announced in the press they made very little impression on the buying public and none have survived today.

Another aspect of motoring in the 1950s was the sidecar which could be attached to scooters as well as to larger capacity motorcycles. Sales of two-wheelers of all types amounted to about a quarter of that of cars, a much higher proportion than today. As a married man added children to his family, there was a need to transport them around and the cheapest way to do this was to add a sidecar to the family scooter or motorcycle. Around a dozen manufacturers in Britain offered a wide range, from lightweight, open single-seaters to enclosed two-seaters with a side door. Design varied from a prewar dated appearance with spoked wheels like the Hillsborough Lonsdale, to fully modern streamlined, pleasant-to-look-at vehicles such as the Watsonian Ascot, which made good use of fibreglass rather than wood in its bodywork.

As the family grew, many scooter owners switched to microcars. There was no legal requirement then to take a test for a different driving licence, and the type of engines used were similar to those of scooters. Road tax was also much cheaper than for a conventional car, plus the vehicles could be purchased for much less. A lot of the advertising of the day showed microcars happily loaded with two children. High performance was beyond the aspirations of the common man so the rather leaden performance of a heavily-laden microcar was simply accepted.

As the 1960s progressed, second-hand conventional cars became more widely available. Their desirability grew as people became better off financially and prices dropped as a result. The sale of scooters and microcars (the latter regarded as a scooter with a roof) gradually declined, even though specification had improved, as had their value for money although the continuing fall in car prices reduced this somewhat. Many well-respected scooter and microcar manufacturers disappeared because of declining sales and, by the end of the 1960s, only the two big scooter manufacturers, Vespa and Lambretta, remained. Microcars as such ceased to be produced or sold in the UK. To enthusiasts this situation was dramatic and barely conceivable! Worse was to follow as, very soon, unbelievably, even the Italian giant Lambretta – a much-respected name in the UK – had gone the way of the rest.

GO man... GO !!

CYCLE and MOTOR CYCLE SHOW
Earls Court 1962

see us on   Stand No. 51 · GROUND FLO
Stand No. 194 · FIRST FLOOR

During the 1970s Japan entered the market and very soon dominated the scene, virtually wiping out the British motorcycle industry with its reliable and much better designed motorcycles, and brilliant series of step-through, partially enclosed small models. These seemed to offer many of the advantages of a scooter with even more reliable modern engines. However, something was lost in the process and the trend toward smaller engines took the life out of scootering.

Later, in the 1980s, a range of small engine capacity scooters arrived from the Far East, illogically going under the name of 'moped', a term formerly used for autocycles, which were really motorised pedal cycles. The pedals were part of the autocycle's design, necessary to propel it up steep gradients. These new, small scooters from the Far East did not have pedals, nor were any necessary as their modern engines were much more powerful; for example, a 50cc engine had the same power as did an earlier 125cc unit. Congestion in city traffic increased the need for more powerful engines to give faste[r] bigger capacity and [...] the word 'scooter' [...] somehow the term [...] its similar small en[...] were reliable but did not offer [...] performance, or inspiration in the styling department, come to that!

The late 1980s witnessed a slow resurgence of the true scooter, this time from Japan and Europe. As demand grew, by the 1990s, it was clear that a second scooter boom was taking place, maybe because many who had appreciated the scooter in their youth yearned to return to them now that their family had grown up.

The designs gradually developed and Italy once again began serious production, to the extent that, today, the country produces more scooters than motorcycles as it did before. France is also back in serious scooter and microcar production and export, with UK sales of the Smart, Aixam and a vehicle from a company called Microcar. Peugeot is responsible for the most popular scooter model. The only other familiar name from the past in the UK is that of Piaggio, parent of Vespa and still going strong with market-leading scooter designs. Britain and Germany have not returned to scooter production despite rumours to the contrary. Japan, however, has been the modern source of most scooter manufacturers and these have established strong reputations as quality motorcycle producers. Other Far Eastern countries enjoy a considerable market share, too. Most of the names of the Taiwanese and Korean scooter manufacturers do not roll off the tongue like the ones we grew up with, but – as happened in the car industry – no doubt they will also become respected and familiar in time as the market continues to grow.

'200'

AMBRETTA and TROJAN

...SORIES and CLUBS

# Scooter clubs and activities

Scooter clubs were a great part of owning a scooter in the 1950s and '60s. There was usually a local evening meeting during the week and an organised club run on Sundays, which toured to places of scenic interest. It was a good way to meet other enthusiasts and to hear about their experiences. It seemed to me that work colleagues were opposed to the very idea of scooters; and in the UK generally these newcomers – considered unstable on the road – met with strong resistance. The idea of rider comfort was dismissed as effeminate and unnecessary. As already mentioned, there was still the feeling that 'British is best' and anything foreign should be considered inferior. The imposition of an import duty on the purchase price further deterred would-be buyers.

The majority of two-wheeler owners were motorcyclists, more numerous, then, than car owners. The full-blown motorcyclist regarded himself as a he-man, and part of that scene was getting oily, grappling with loose chains – and the consumption of alcohol! Scooterists, on the other hand, were much more refined: social drinking was part of their scene, too, but it was more likely to be coffee!

The Sunday club run was good fun and a way of showing off your pride and joy: a row of scooters in convoy always attracted the attention of passers-by and were often greeted by cheery waves and smiles.

There were usually at least half-a-dozen scooters on the runs which increased to double that figure in the summer months. Of course, there was so much more room on the roads then that it was quite safe and practical for the last scooter in the line, called tail-end Charlie, to overtake and run up and down the line keeping everyone together, often halting the run if anyone had to stop because of mechanical trouble. (A common occurrence as many new owners had little

No, not that Pennsylvania. Members of the Continentals, a Bristol scooter club, pose at a village roadside sign north of Bath in 1962.

What fun! A Lambretta Starstream and a Heinkel bubblecar on Brean Down in Somerset.

*Some of the author's past scooter collection.*

mechanical knowledge, and some of the designs had not had time to develop reliability.) Vehicles were generally not as reliable then as those we take for granted today.

Scooter clubs would organise and run sporting events such as gymkhanas, treasure hunts, navigation trials and long-distance rallies, not only for their own members but for those in other clubs, too. Associations, such as the National Scooter Association which was made up of members from many different clubs, were established nationally to coordinate these activities. National clubs were also set up by manufacturers, particularly for people who had purchased one of their products. Perhaps the best of these in the UK was the British Lambretta Owners Association which was able to provide the best facilities for members, although the Vespa Club of Great Britain also did a fine job. Some of the smaller producers, such as NSU and Puch, also had national clubs. Others, like DKR, produced a nice chromium owners club badge but little else!

As sales increased so did the facilities for members. Large petrol companies staged events for scooters, such as the Esso Scoot to Scotland, and there were economy runs to show off what mileage could be achieved by using a particular brand of two-stroke petroil mix. The grandest scooter event of the year was the Isle of Man Scooter Rally which attracted not only the usual scooterist and his family but also teams of serious riders from many manufacturers. The rally was a week of special events for scooter riders which usually followed on from the Isle of Man TT motorcycle races. Of particular note was the 24 hour endurance run which was very effective in demonstrating the reliability of various makes. It was a good place to be for the enthusiast, who could see a great range in action rather than just looking at a static line of machines in a dealer's showroom. It was also good to meet owners of other makes and talk about their scooters and the relative benefits and drawbacks.

# Bristol Scooter Club
## The Continentals

### 1961

# Scooter magazines

*Scooter World* was a very go-ahead magazine which first appeared in December 1955. It became *the* voice of the scooter enthusiast and was justifiably very popular. The photos it published were large and clear, and there were many interesting letters from owners, plus it had information on all the emerging new designs. The magazine offered free yellow windscreen stickers of "The Office Cat", which were very popular and seen on scooters and crash helmets all around the country.

*Scooter and Threewheeler* was the second bestseller, smaller in format but thicker. It attracted more advertisers than did *Scooter World,* probably because it was not so outspoken editorially. If *Scooter World*, didn't like something about a scooter or a company, it said so, and then lost its advertising! *Scooter and Threewheeler* magazine hardly ever criticized a machine in its road tests and, in that respect, did potential owners a disservice, but continued to receive advertising!

There was also an established moped magazine called *Power and Pedal* which began to include scooters. That periodical started life in 1952 when the boom in sales of power-assisted pedal cycles began in the UK. The moped developed from these, with frames and brakes especially designed to be motor driven. Somehow, *Power and Pedal*'s publisher managed to sell this good magazine for just sixpence, which was very good value, and half the cover price of *Scooter World*. Scooterists had greater affinity with mopeds than motorcycles, although they did want more power and style than these machines offered.

Scooterists very much appreciated having their own magazines when they arrived, not really having any liking for or interest in the long-established motorcycle magazines such as *The Motorcycle* and *Motorcycling*, whose readers thought that scooters were an oddity, and only a passing fad in any case. In their opinion nothing could match conventional motorcycles; why cover over the mechanics that needed to be worked on, adding weight and making it quieter? The noise was part of the he-man ethos! Little wheels were bound to be unsafe, and fancy designing a machine like the Vespa with the engine on one side; it can't be good for stability! (They may have had a point there, although in practice it was never borne out.) *Motorcycling* did eventually soften its attitude and included a separate section at the back, printed on yellow pages and called *Scooter Weekly*. However, after a time, as the size of the section grew, white paper was used as it was easier to read the copy. Few scooterists bought a motorcycle magazine just to read a few pages at the back, however.

Much later the section gained its independence and emerged as a weekly newspaper. In this form, however, photographs were not presented at their best. Scooterists are and were very interested in style and how their machines looked, and most wanted

NINEPENCE
MONTHLY
December 1961

VOL X    No I

# Classic

# SCOOTER

The present with the future

to keep their magazines for reference. Eventually, a new, separate glossy magazine was produced, printed on good paper: *Scooter Weekly* magazine was born.

*Scooter News* then appeared, and also *Practical Scooter and Moped*. *Scooter News* expanded and added *Mechanics* to its title. *Power and Pedal* became *The Scooter with Power and Pedal* as the market evolved and mopeds lost popularity.

Under new management *Scooter World*

became *Scooter and Lightweights* at a time when scooter sales were declining in an effort to increase readership by including some light motorcycles in its coverage. The two didn't mix very well and eventually – after little more than a decade – unbelievably, all of the major dedicated scooter magazines had faded away.

October 1967 was a terrible period for enthusiasts as *Scooter and Threewheeler* and *Practical Scooter* ceased publication for ever. The former magazine was market leader and, with its demise, the future of scooters and microcars seemed in grave jeopardy. Some motorcycle magazines pledged to

*A Messerschmitt cabin scooter at Crich in Derbyshire.*

cover the scooter scene from then on, and did feature occasional articles. But as sales continued to decline, all mention of scooters ceased.

Microcar owners – with lower sales volumes – had had to be satisfied with occasional mentions in scooter and motor magazines. Even *Scooter and Threewheeler* would go several issues without mention of microcars or three-wheelers. *Power and Pedal* did feature a microcar section for a while under the title *Three-wheeler News*. Microcar sales fell away with those of scooters – perhaps even more sharply – and car magazines gave up featuring articles about them.

Only Lambretta and Vespa continued to manufacture scooters, and then with limited availability. These machines seemed to attract a different type of individual and, by the time the Mods appeared in the late 1960s, scooters were not owned by the same sort of people they had been in the 1950s.

From time to time over the following years, magazines for scooterists would start up; brave efforts which soon faded away. Especially remembered are *Scootering World, The British Scooterist Scene* and *Scooter Maniac*. Some were produced at home and only available by postal subscription. A few microcar and scooter owner's club magazines did continue for their members, playing a vital role in keeping alive the spark of interest. Vespa and Lambretta still had many devoted fans, as did Bond, Heinkel, Isetta and Messerschmitt in the microcar world, even though production of these machines had long since ceased. Specialist scooter dealers became experts at finding machines and microcar owner's clubs were able to scour the world to find spares and reproduce them to keep their machines working. The importation and restoration of old scooters and, to a lesser degree, microcars began. There was still a place for them on the roads.

The mid-1980s saw several appealing new two-wheeler designs emerge to challenge the dull, low powered, so-called step-throughs and erroneously named mopeds which dominated the market. Aprilia of Italy introduced to the UK market the very sleek-looking and relatively powerful 125cc Leonardo, with performance equivalent to that of 200cc scooters in the 1950s, plus a large and very comfortable saddle. Also from Italy came the Malaguti Yesterday, a retro design with whitewall tyres and chrome features – style had returned to scootering – and a very useful storage locker at the rear. The search was on to find solutions to growing traffic congestion. As sales of the new machines increased, so, too, did interest and gradually machines which resembled the scooter of old appeared from Japan and Europe. This time round they were even more user-friendly; gone was the messy business of mixing oil with petrol, petrol taps and fiddly chokes.

A new magazine – *Scooterscene* – was launched as sales of, and interest in, scooters escalated. Later,

another magazine called *Scootering* appeared and these two eventually merged as *Scootering* took over *Scooterscene*. The new magazine was really an enlarged version of *Scooterscene* and soon contained so much material each month that it had to resort to small-sized print and small photos to get it all in!

*Scootering* soon became the most successful scooter magazine ever with an increasing international readership. In recent times it has spawned a spin-off magazine called *Twist and Go* which concentrates on the modern automatic scooters. The title is symbolic of how easy it is to drive the modern scooter.

*Scootering* continues to cover all aspects of scooter ownership, ancient and modern, including (to my mind) a more bizarre music and lifestyle scene compared to the original 1950s world of scootering.

Occasional articles about microcars do feature but, so far, the range and popularity of these machines has not matched that of the scooter.

# Picture gallery

A DKR Capella outside a modern office block near Filton in Bristol.

The yellow of this Dayton Flamenco complements the springtime scene at Horfield Common in Bristol.

An Agrati Capri on the headland at West Bay in Dorset.

A Lambretta Rallymaster at Weston-super-Mare, Somerset.

A Prior scooter at the headland near Portreath in Cornwall.

A newly-restored Zundapp Bella at a VMSC fun day.

A Vespa GS at a park in Milton Keynes, Buckinghamshire.

Admiring a Durkopp Diana at the Chantry Kilve in west Somerset.

that's lux

...all the features you've always wanted—and never found before

A Vespa 125 at a transport rally in Cheltenham, Gloucestershire.

a *Diana*

...rfection and for perfection—that is

Enthusiasts discuss the merits of the Lambretta Li series 1.

A Maico Maicomobile with period diesel locomotive and train at Crowcombe Heathfield station in west Somerset.

A Durkopp Diana TS at dusk at Watchet in west Somerset

A Vespa 180 SS and Scammel three-wheeler lorry at a transport rally, Castle Combe in Wiltshire.

The line-up of scooters at a VMSC fun day in Enderby, Leicestershire.

A Durkopp Diana Sport at a mill near Upper Slaughter in Oxfordshire.

A Lambretta SX beside a fine example of a period Bristol Eastern National coach.

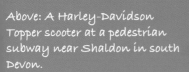

Above: A Harley-Davidson Topper scooter at a pedestrian subway near Shaldon in south Devon.

Above right: An Adler scooter and a 1965 Vauxhall Victor 101 estate at Sibley Back reservoir in Cornwall.

Right: A Lambretta Super Starstream scooter near the grand pier at Weston-super-Mare in Somerset.

A Honda Stream and Ariel Three with Burgh Island in south Devon as a backdrop.

A Lambretta J125 at Knightstone, Weston-super-Mare, Somerset.

A Moby 150 and period
Bedford OB coach at
Newport in south Wales.

A Lambretta SX at
Cothelstone Manor,
west Somerset.

The Peugeot Elite scooter has extra storage within its front mudguard.

Lambretta Li series 1 – and matching house!

Above: A Cyclemaster Piatti (left) and Dayton Albatross.

Taking the sea air in Clevedon, Somerset, is this Rumi Little Ant scooter.

Lambretta GP scooters attend a rally at
Kesterfield near Northlew in north Devon.

A Sun Wasp scooter at Blists
Hill in Shropshire.

A Vespa Rally 180 amid the rolling hills of Challaborough in south Devon.

Below: Heinkel A1 scooters at a microcar rally near Milton Keynes in Buckinghamshire.

A Velocette Viceroy on the headland at Ilfracombe in north Devon.

The scooter line-up at anoth[er]
VMSC fun day at Enderby
Leicestershi[re]

# Evolution

The early seventies were depressing times for scooter and microcar enthusiasts. People generally had better buying power, and with conventional cars becoming cheaper and more plentiful, more and more were upgrading to these and no longer buying scooters and microcars. Values plummeted and few were seen on the roads.

I kept my Dayton scooter until 1974, but only as a second means of transport. When I no longer had a garage to keep it in I decided it would be better to sell the scooter than leave it out in the open under a plastic cover. All I could get for it was £10, and I had to knock a pound off that to clinch the deal! Ten years later I spent a hundred times that amount restoring another Dayton of the same model, so I very much regret letting my original go for such a song. Actually finding one to restore wasn't easy, either!

Looking back, it was good that Lambretta and Vespa did manage to survive when so many other makes faded away. Those who continued to ride them were the keenest enthusiasts, and their machines were lavished with care, which is why so many examples of these two makes are still around today. Vespa and Lambretta were the reasons why scootering became so popular in the UK in the early1950s. However, as a scootering teenager then, I didn't realise that about a decade earlier, British-designed scooters – such as the Swallow Gadabout – were being made and sold in the UK. Even earlier than this there had been others like the Townsend Autoglider, and earlier still the Unibus, designed,

made and sold in the UK in the 1920s, which could well claim to be the first true scooter.

In the microcar world the Scootacar – a microcar calling itself a scootercar – was made by Rytecraft long before the more familiar Hunslet Scootacar appeared. (Microcars in general had existed but not under that collective title.)

In the 1970s, some enlightened individuals began to stockpile scooters and microcars as they went out of fashion. These had very little monetary value, so the idea was to preserve the machines, or use them as a source of spares to keep their machines, or those of friends, on the road. It was nice to ride something different still, something with links to the past.

It was hard to understand what was happening to the world of scootering. In the 1950s when scooters first appeared in earnest, scooterists believed that their machines would mean the end of conventional motorcycles, apart from the fastest, but now our machines were waning, too. The British motorcycle industry was also dying, due, in no small part, to the Japanese-made machines now flooding our markets. Besides superior motorcycles, Japan sent us step-through, part-covered vehicles that weren't true scooters, but soon saw off all competition anyway, mainly because of their cost efficiency and great reliability which took the idea of convenient economic transport to a new level. In the eyes of the enthusiast, however, they looked more like covered motorcycles and, as such, were not welcomed with enthusiasm by the traditional scooterist.

In the 1980s I had been attracted to the idea of owning various Japanese tiny-wheeled, so-called mopeds from Honda and Suzuki, for the sake of convenience, but somehow they did not have the appeal of genuine scooters. Their even smaller, narrow wheels could easily slide sideways in bad conditions, although it was nice to have strong plastic bodywork which did not rust or show scratches!

Those who remembered the great variety of scooters of old missed them and their unique style, fearing they would be lost for ever.

As the eighties progressed, more and more people took up restoration of these machines from the past, and they began to appear at classic vehicle rallies and shows, providing something different and evoking fond memories for many who saw them. The situation with microcars was the same and this is what brought me back into the scene. Contact was made with like-minded enthusiasts; machines were dragged out of the back of sheds and barns, and spares were swopped. Gradually, a representative range of 1950s and '60s scooters and microcars built up around the UK.

I spent ten years finding and restoring some of these machines, which gave me a lot of pleasure and satisfaction. I started with just one, a Heinkel bubblecar, as it was the first to come my way, but soon built up a reasonable collection of scooters, too. A sudden, adverse change in personal finances brought a halt to my restorations, sadly, forcing me to sell what I had spent time and money recreating.

*Och aye, the noo. A Lambretta LD equipped with tartan accessories.*

During the wilderness years of the seventies, the Lambretta and Vespa owner's clubs kept together the nucleus of enthusiasts. Scooter magazines came along and died away but, with the arrival of *Scooterscene* (later to merge with *Scootering*), a great, popular publication with growing circulation was born, which retained links with the past whilst promoting the present and future.

During the 1980s, clubs – such as the Vintage Motor Scooter Club – were formed and helped to accelerate the restoration hobby, putting enthusiasts in touch with one another and staging events and shows. Also at this time the second scooter boom began, with interesting designs coming from Japan and also Europe. These machines were very much more efficient and attractive than those we had grown up with, offering a lot of convenience for a little money. Increasing congestion on overcrowded roads made the machines seem attractive and useful again, and they were so much more user-friendly than the originals. Now, it was possible to have a scooter which didn't need to have oil mixed with petrol at every fill-up; petrol taps no longer had to be turned on and off, and crash helmets could be conveniently and safely stowed within the scooter when not required.

Microcars, too, reappeared in a much more civilised and user-friendly form. With the exception of the Smart – a brilliant, thoroughly modern microcar – they still have some way to go to achieve mass popularity, although the modern scooter is fully accepted and a useful machine. UK sales of other modern microcars from Aixam, Ligier, and the French concern which calls itself simply Microcar, have so far been modest. The new microcar, MC1, however, is seen on the roads in ever-increasing numbers, as it – like the Smart – does offer the option of some

The Honda Melody, a typical example of a 1970s Japanese, 'moped'.

luxury items as well as economy. The modern microcar would benefit from further development, especially in a reduction of purchase price. Modern safety regulations do, unfortunately, add cost and restrictions to simple designs. Mass production manufacture of conventional cars still gives them the edge in terms of value for money when compared to microcars.

Looking back, it is difficult to imagine a time when scooters and microcars were virtually unseen on Britain's roads; with so much congestion, the demand today for something small and economic has never been greater. The future looks bright indeed for these fine and interesting machines.

# Classic scooter profiles

This chapter takes a closer look at a selection of popular makes and models. There is some nostalgic detail about what it was like to own and use one. The sort of person who owned them was special, too, and contemporary adverts provided a good visual portrayal of scooter and microcar people and the world they lived in.

Photographs of the machines in typical surroundings, together with manufacturer sales material, complete the picture. Some of the photos feature other classic vehicles from the same period, whilst still others have been taken in scenic situations.

Today, these sales brochures are very collectable and – even if copies can be located – are expensive to purchase. Most are no longer available.

Specification details and sales information appears later in the book with more typical period adverts and brochures.

### Brockhouse Corgi

When you are growing up, what you see and hear around you can have a big influence. When attending primary school in the late 1940s, I would see buses, lorries, cars and motorcycles on the roads. Only one person living in our street actually owned a car; I was told that only rich people could afford one of those!

Buses were transport for the masses and the usual means of getting about. To me they appeared to be smart, comfortable, friendly creations that took you anywhere you wanted to go at prices you could afford. They regularly stopped at the end of our street, and took us into town and to other buses or trains if we needed to travel further afield.

Plymouth, the city where I grew up, had the benefit of a good bus company which really looked after its buses, keeping the very smart red and cream livery clean and polished. I came to recognise the various different makes and models and chose my favourites amongst them. Many were prewar designs with an efficient, rugged appeal. All were British designed and produced.

Cars were mostly boring and available only in black, as were motorcycles. Someone owned a motorcycle in the next street, but what I saw of it did not impress me greatly. It was an ancient-looking thing that was oily and made a lot of noise. If you

... and on a garden lawn at
Washford in west Somerset.

touched it, you either burnt yourself or got dirty marks on your clothing. I was told to keep away from it!

Whenever its owner rode this machine he was unrecognizable, wearing a long black coat and battle helmet, and an elastic thing on his face with holes cut in it for the eyes. To start the machine a lot of physical effort was necessary just to pull it off the stand. Then it had to be repeatedly kicked. When finally it started, the noise was deafening to little ears. Sometimes, the motorcyclist would take someone with him on the back, and they always appeared to be hanging on for grim death, wrapping their arms around him to keep from falling off. As it finally departed it left in its wake a trail of smoke and pools of oil. It seemed to my young eyes to be some sort of wild mechanical horse, complete with hot, spinning, oily bits between your legs. "I don't like motorcycles at all", I thought!

Of course, I have since grown to appreciate the different

# *Folding* CORGI *Portable*

## MOTOR CYCLE

### 98 c.c.     KICK START

The **CORGI** is powered by the famous Brockhouse "Spryt" engine and the design features practical streamlining. It has parking head and tail lights—hand and foot brakes—kick and push start—ample capacity gravity feed fuel tank—150 miles from one filling—120 m.p.g.—30 m.p.h. with ease—weight 95 lbs.

**EASY TO RIDE** in town and/or country—at work or play, there's scarcely a limit to the usefulness of the CORGI for every person who requires compact, efficient and ECONOMICAL transport.

**IT'S SMALL—BUT IT'S TERRIFIC.**

**PRICE: £52**

plus Purchase Tax £14 . 0 . 10

Sole Concessionaires for Great Britain, Northern Ireland, Channel Islands, Eire, France and Spain.

# JACK OLDING & CO. LTD.    Tel. Mayfair 5242

## AUDLEY HOUSE, NORTH AUDLEY STREET, MAYFAIR, W.1

mechanical approach to motoring that motorcycles offer, though still feel that they are generally rather uncivilised!

Although there were no scooters on the road, there was an interesting little disc-wheeled machine I occasionally saw called a Corgi. "That looks a lot friendlier" I mused. The rider was perched high above the mechanical bits and, instead of roaring, it purred. "I quite like those" I thought. (A few years later I saw my first Vespa and that was me hooked.) The Corgi was a peacetime development of a wartime paratroopers' fold-up motorcycle, designed to be dropped by parachute. These were called Welbikes after Welwyn, where they were designed. They had little Villiers engines and were built under license by Excelsior.

After the war a firm called Brockhouse Engineering decided to develop these for peacetime use on the roads, and, for the Corgi, produced a two-stroke engine similar to the Villiers used in the Welbike.

Excelsior modelled the Corgi on previous designs. Lights were fitted together with mudguards; the original spoked wheels were replaced by disc wheels, and the fuel tank located on top of the engine rather than beside it. It had a simple rubber squeeze bulb horn. It could still be folded up – the handlebar stems were unclipped and laid down horizontally over the fuel tank and the saddle stem retracted within itself  to store in a small space, such as the boot of a reasonably large car.

The Corgi was capable of speeds up to around 30mph and the brakes were reasonable. Lighting was dim, but at least you could be seen by other road users! Advertising claimed it was possible to cover 125 miles at a cost in fuel of 2/6d. The Corgi could be purchased for £66.

The Corgi appeared in different forms between 1948 and the mid-50s, eventually getting a two-speed gearbox instead of just one. It received a kickstarter instead of having to rely on a push-start; sprung front suspension and a luggage carrier fitted on top of the fuel tank. Commercial models had a box sidecar fitted to an extended frame. Finally, some weather protection was built in to the front end but not at all stylishly. Some were exported and, in the US, they were sold briefly as the Indian Papoose.

When the first Vespas and Lambrettas appeared the Corgi was no competition and sales nose-dived. Instead of developing the little machine in competition, Excelsior simply gave up and production

ceased, although it did try developing the engine to 125cc, but without success. This is a shame as the Corgi could well have carried a smooth body with a larger engine and been very similar to the Piatti which followed in 1958.

How ironic that the Corgi originated from a machine designed to assist in the defeat of Germany and Italy in wartime, later to be sidelined in peacetime by scooters from these very countries ...

### BSA Sunbeam & Triumph Tigress

This was the machine that achieved belated acceptance of the scooter by the British motorcycle industry. Traditional manufacturers had been rather reluctant to accept that the scooter had a place in the transport scene, but, as more and more people purchased machines from abroad, they finally got the message.

As early as 1955, BSA had produced a design for a scooter, calling it the Beeza. Prototypes were shown at the Earls Court Show, sales leaflets were produced and magazin articles appeared heralding this great leap forward. Then – nothing. BSA got cold feet and decided not to go ahead with production, which was probably just as well as the design was expensive and based on a sidevalve engine, and therefore very much out of date.

In 1958 the Sunbeam scooter was announced and this time BSA was serious about the project. The scooter was reasonably priced but took a while to woo the buying public which, by this time, had been led to believe and understand that the best scooters

A BSA Sunbeam on the headland at Croyde Bay in north Devon ...

were good, but the designer provided nothing in the way of storage – not even enough for a pair of gloves. A steering lock was provided but initially no ignition key, meaning the engine could be started by any passer-by, a failing not rectified until the mid-1960s.

Chain drive was employed, running within an oil bath chaincase: very good in theory, but leaking oil in practice. A four-speed gearbox was fitted which was operated by a single foot pedal. There was a separate neutral selector which was similar to that on the very successful Durkopp Diana. BSA

came from Italy and Germany.

The decision to call the same scooter both BSA (Sunbeam) and Triumph (Tigress) caused confusion. In actual fact, the design had come from the Triumph factory which had become part of BSA. (Something similar was happening in the car industry for no logical reason.) The BSA was coloured green and the Triumph blue. Tigress was arguably the better name, as Sunbeam was still for many associated with an earlier larger motorcycle. However, the new scooter was designed as a whole within the same company and not a collection of bolt-together parts from various sources, a criticism of most British designs. Styling was individual and smooth, spoilt only by the rear number plate and lamp, essential items which appeared to have been overlooked in the planning stage. In order to fit a rear carrier it was necessary to remove the plate and lamp and bolt on behind!

BSA had been right in its choice of a relatively large 250cc, four-stroke engine, but seriously wrong in designing side panels that required several different sized spanners, and half an hour's patience to remove. If a carrier or spare wheel was fitted to the scooter, this, too, had to be removed first in order to undo the side panels. To be fair to the design, a small removable panel allowed access to the clutch adjustment and points, but other engine items were not at all easy to get at.

Engine performance, ride quality and braking

also wisely followed that machine's example of retaining the kickstart on electric starter versions. (The starter was a car-type rather than a dynastart system as on most other scooters.)

The engine always ran very hot, causing many problems, and the side panels literally became too hot to touch. Only much later in the production run was the silencer removed from within the bodyshell and placed under the front mudguard. Early stands were easy to use but would not hold the machine on a slope. The wheels were retained by just three bolts – four being the norm – but tyre levers were required to get the tyre off in the event of a puncture. Production quality control was not good and many owners had continual problems with broken components and oil leaks.

Advertising and aftersales were good and many machines found overseas buyers based on BSA's past reputation. Even some performance records were broken by the scooters but always in a stripped-down form without side panels and with a saddle tied on with string!

A 175cc, single cylinder, two-stroke version followed based on the BSA Bantam motorcycle engine, a copy of a prewar German DKW engine but was not as successful. It wasn't much cheaper to purchase, performance was not as good, and fuel consumption not much better than the larger 250cc version.

Both machines suffered for having a small

THE
SCOOTER
THAT HAS
EVERYTHING!

**BSA SUNBEAM**

B.S.A. MOTOR CYCLES LTD.
415 WAVERLEY WORKS
BIRMINGHAM 11

fuel tank, and the engine would not run with a low fuel level. Batteries were fitted in metal boxes on the legshields; two for 12v electric start versions and one for 6v kickstart models. Often, these boxes corroded and the batteries could not be accessed, causing even more aggravation.

Production of both models ended in 1965, the four-stroke disappearing first during a very unsettling period for the motorcycle and scooter industries. Japanese imports were swamping the market, forcing many old established firms to close due to lack of business, including, eventually, BSA/Triumph.

## Dayton Albatross

When, in the late 1940s, Italy was gearing up to produce worldclass motorscooters, the British motorcycle industry simply stood by and poured scorn on the idea that a large percentage of two-wheeler owners wanted weather protection and style without the need for special clothing.

Very soon Germany, Austria and France, amongst others, were producing their own scooter designs, and sales were rocketing. The British industry again did nothing, until it became very obvious that motorcycle sales were dropping off.

Then, in the early fifties, one or two of the big names in motorcycle manufacture produced some scooter prototypes, which were unveiled at shows, although in most cases production models did not follow. Not all of the industry turned a blind eye, however, and in 1954 the Dayton Cycle Company of London – which, before the war, had made motorcycles – took the decision to invest heavily in the production of a relatively high powered motor scooter with conservative British suspension and braking system. Unfortunately, however, the message had not fully hit home as styling was not high on the priorities.

The first model – the Albatross – appeared on the market in 1956 and, though good in mechanical design, did not

A 1959 Dayton Albatross with fine example of a period Bristol Southern National coach.

satisfy the very real need for style. The efficient front suspension worked well enough, but looked awful: all exposed ironwork topped by a basic motorcycle-type mudguard; the front legshields were flat and unaerodynamic, and handlebars were unshielded, motorcycle-style. In performance, however, the Albatross was good and received good reviews in the motorcycle press. And it did keep its rider clean!

Another bad move by Dayton was to virtually ignore the several motor scooter magazines now in existence, preferring to send occasional update publicity to *The Motor Cycle,* a magazine hardly ever read by scooterists! Dayton's attitude was that a good machine sells itself; no truer then than it is today. Just how much of the design was original is debatable, because

A Dayton Albatross at a Messerschmitt rally in Kingham, Oxfordshire.

expensive to buy than the competition, and probably too heavy for the mass market. It did benefit from gradual improvements, including side pannier bags – again a motorcycle-type idea – rather than having an enclosed compartment within the scooter, as a scooterist would prefer.

Extra chromework was added to the front mudguard, but it wasn't until 1958 that the front suspension was fully enclosed and the machine began to look more attractive. Sales did then increase and the famous Villiers 2T 250cc, twin two-stroke engine became the standard for the Dayton. This excellent British engine gave greater performance and economy with the bonus of a very pleasant purring sound in operation.

In early 1959, front styling was again improved, with curved legshields and an even more aerodynamic front mudguard. A useful front glovebox was added. By this time the scooter market had really opened up in the UK with a choice of over 60 models, including

it very closely followed the shape of the German Zundapp Bella, using a tunnel between the rider's feet to duct cooling air over a standard motorcycle engine. (It could be argued that the Bella resembled the earlier Italian Parilla, so I suppose everything is relative!)

The Albatross was a very good rider's scooter, with ease of engine maintenance, good performance and braking, good economy and a comfortable ride. It originally used the Villiers 2H 225cc, single cylinder, two-stroke engine, later changed to the Villiers 250cc, single cylinder unit. The entire rear bodywork could be released clear of the engine by removal of four nuts and two bolts.

As the company did not advertise the model, the new generation of scooter riders did not read about it in their magazines, so demand was not high. You couldn't miss Lambretta and Vespa advertising if you tried, but most young people had never heard of Dayton. The Albatross was also much more

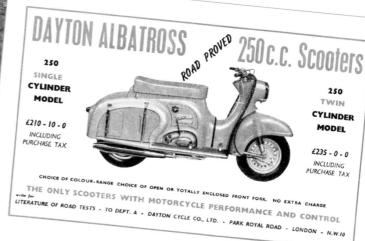

**DAYTON ALBATROSS** *ROAD PROVED* **250 c.c. Scooters**

250 SINGLE CYLINDER MODEL

£210 - 10 - 0 INCLUDING PURCHASE TAX

250 TWIN CYLINDER MODEL

£235 - 0 - 0 INCLUDING PURCHASE TAX

CHOICE OF COLOUR-RANGE CHOICE OF OPEN OR TOTALLY ENCLOSED FRONT FORK. NO EXTRA CHARGE

**THE ONLY SCOOTERS WITH MOTORCYCLE PERFORMANCE AND CONTROL**

write for LITERATURE OF ROAD TESTS - TO DEPT. A - DAYTON CYCLE CO., LTD. · PARK ROYAL ROAD · LONDON · N.W.10

DAYTON SCOOTERS hold a special place in the affections of those who love the open road, whether it be in town, in country or at the seaside. The smart, comfort-built lines of Dayton scooters put them way ahead in any crowd. Designed for maximum reliability, with the highest possible performance, they combine economy both in running and maintenance costs.

some from the larger British motorcycle companies. There was only so much money about, so to keep its machine in the running Dayton added a full width glovebox and fully enclosed handlebars.

If only the scooter had started out that way in 1954, with good publicity it could have been a real winner. By 1960, however, the company experienced financial difficulties when it took over a rival which was greatly in debt. It had been hoped to expand production with more factory space but, sadly, like a lot of other British companies at that time, Dayton went out of business.

Today, about 20 preserved Albatrosses exist, many belonging to former owners who remember their scooters with great affection and pride. It was one of the best scooters of the fifties, and British, which dared to suggest that scooters need not be limited to about-town performance.

## DKR

DKR was one of the more go-ahead British scooter companies, and identified the need for a British scooter much earlier than established motorcycle companies. With the aid of Willenhall Motor Radiators, which produced the bodywork, and Villiers, which supplied the engines, work began in 1956 and production followed in 1957.

The initials DKR are an acronym of the initials of the three directors of the firm: Day, Kieft and Robinson. Kieft had a background in car racing and, in 1956, began importing the German Hercules scooter, selling it under his own name. The Hercules was a very successful design which sold for a relatively high price (the name of this machine was later to change when sold to Prior in the UK).

Kieft realised that if he could fit the locally-made Villiers engine rather than the German Sachs, the scooter could be sold for less. In 1957 he fitted a Villiers engine in a Hercules and carried out a long-distance trial to evaluate the arrangement. His next step was to design a body for the scooter. The rear half was a virtual copy of the Hercules, perhaps under license, but for the front he decided to fit the fuel tank ahead of the steering column, rather than behind, as

in the case of the Hercules. This improved the weight balance and freed up space for a useful storage locker within the legshields. The shape of the front was an acquired taste, not appealing to all, and rather reminiscent of a large Roman nose! (The Austrian KTM Mirabell used the same idea with much more stylish results.)

In 1958 the first DKR scooter – called the DKR Dove – went on sale. Its front end was practical and aerodynamic but gave it an unbalanced look, especially without a carrier which made the rear appear smaller than the front. The engine and its kickstarter were located very high in the frame, making starting awkward and difficult; later, an electric starter version, the DKR Pegasus, arrived, followed by the 200cc DKR Defiant still with the same bodywork. Top-of-the-range was a 250cc twin cylinder with a fan-cooled Villiers 2T engine. This had plenty of power but the cooling system was not adequate and the fan cowlings made engine access difficult.

A special 325cc version was produced to generate publicity which could take a passenger in a sidecar and tow a small caravan on a journey to Gibraltar and back, a feat which earned it good publicity. This same engine was later used in some British microcars.

In 1960, DKR decided to employ the services of an industrial artist who came up with the design of what many consider to be the best-looking British scooter, the DKR Capella.

It did not offer any storage space within the bodywork apart from enough for a small tool roll. It did, however, look very appealing; a very important consideration in the scootering world. The body lines were smooth, elegant and practical, and it even made the current stylish Lambrettas look outdated.

The Capella received good press reviews and sales were buoyant. It became available with a good range of different capacity engines, both kickstart and electric. The design of the rear wheel meant that it could be easily and quickly removed in case of a puncture, unlike its predecessor, which was awful! On all the previous models apart from the latest, the chain had to be split to get the wheel off. I owned a Defiant in 1959 and, on one long, dreadful

The DKR Capella (left) evolved from the DKR Dove (middle) which, in turn, evolved from a Kieft.

A DKR Capella (centre) at an indoor VMSC scooter show at Gloucester.

winter journey, experienced three punctures due to a defective tube, which was a nightmare. The Capella retained the more complicated dual leg front suspension, but the wheel there could be removed by pulling out a central spindle. This leading link suspension did allow a smooth ride and a non-dip braking experience.

In theory the Capella could have been a world beater if it had been released years earlier at the time of the Dove, rather than appearing just as car sales were escalating and scooter sales declining. The Capella did sell in reasonable numbers in the UK, however, and probably was the most successful British design from small company.

Design criticisms are few.

Pretty, pastel-coloured Ducati Brios on North Hill, in Minehead, west Somerset (unfortunately, not on speaking terms ...).

A 1964 Ducati Brio 100 ready for the off near Liverpool; the only city in which the model was sold.

Firstly, access to the sparkplug was not good. It appeared that later on in the design it was necessary to fit engine stabilising bars inside the purpose-built sparkplug flap, which impeded access. Another gripe was the amazingly complex dual flow fuel pipes and tap which got in the way of access to the carburettor. A special, long-reach oil can was also needed to top up the primary chaincase. Visually, the rear wheel would have looked much cleaner if the chain guard had also enclosed the chain adjusters. It didn't look too bad when clean and new, but as soon as it became dirty in use, it was not an attractive sight.

The Capella demonstrated that Britain *could* come up with a stylish, up-to-the-minute scooter that was reasonably priced, well supported, reliable, and appealing to look at.

It was a sad day when DKR finally closed in the mid-1960s. Even then the Capella still looked appealing and modern.

## Ducati

Most UK scooter enthusiasts were unaware of the Ducati Brio scooter as it was only very briefly imported to Britain for a few months in 1965, and again fleetingly in 1968.

Back in Italy, Ducati was a much-respected producer of scooters and motorcycles. Its first scooter was called the Cruiser and appeared in 1952. This was revolutionary in that it used a car-type automatic gearbox. The four-stroke engine was 175cc, and equipped with an electric starter. Side panels hinged open from the rear for unhindered access to everything mechanical. The prototypes proved too powerful for the then current regulations, so the production scooters had to be detuned and a restrictor

fitted in the silencer, which caused some problems with smooth running. This, and a high retail price, meant that the Cruiser did not find a large market, a great shame as it was a truly magnificent scooter, both visually and mechanically. If only it could have been further developed and exported to the UK it would have found many buyers here, as scooterists in this country have always appreciated the more powerful machines, unlike those in Italy who considered that economy was most important.

Sadly, Ducati ceased production of the Cruiser in 1954 and did not venture back into scooters until 1963. This time the company went to the opposite extreme and tried to design a very simple and basic scooter. Fan cooling was added to an existing, well-developed motorcycle engine of 48cc, which had a three-speed gearchange operated by a handlebar twistgrip, and conventional open chain drive. The wheels were nine inch with split rims. Electrics were six volt ac with no battery. It did, however, possess a simple charm that brought it success in its home market. The scooter was named Brio which means

flair, or brightness. It continued in production for several years.

In 1964 a larger version of the Brio was produced using a different 94cc motorcycle engine, again modified to fan cooling. At first glance the body appeared identical to that used on the 48cc version, but when placed side-by-side the so-called Brio 100 was slightly higher and longer. It also had a longer dualseat and was fitted with eight inch wheels, probably to make it easier to fit a more common tyre size. The official colour was a pale green but creamy white ones have also been seen.

In 1967 the 48cc Brio was renamed Brio 50 but the name badge was the only change. It was still only officially available in a creamy white colour but recent evidence suggests that some blue ones were produced. Some examples show a slight change in the angle of the panel ahead of the engine, perhaps to increase accessibility.

Also in 1967 the Brio 100 was renamed 100/25, but again the only difference was the badge. The larger-engined Brio sold better than the smaller version though both were discontinued in 1968.

The Brios imported to the UK in 1968 were heavily discounted in order to clear the factory at the end of production. They were purchased by a single dealer in Liverpool and only available from this source.

Today, Ducati motorcycle owners feel the same way about the Ducati Brio as BMW car drivers do about the Isetta bubblecar: both would rather forget they ever existed ...

## Durkopp Diana

In 1956 when I was first drawn to motor scooters, there were many interesting and attractive machines on the market, and a great range of prices, some very much more out of reach than others! Among the dearest was the German Diana, a machine with many attractive features, some of which were unique, such as the one-pedal gearchange and neutral selector. Italian scooters ruled the roost, primarily for their style and reliability, but the Diana was a match in both respects.

Generally, German scooters tended to be heavy and bulky in appearance, but the Diana's simple, flowing lines set it apart. It offered good weather protection and practical features, together with a certain elegance. Starting was by kickstart, or, provided as standard, an electric dynastarter, thanks to the Noris 12v electrics. The kickstarter was special, however, as the pedal could also be used to select neutral by a simple prod of the left heel. Gear changing was via a single short travel foot pedal pushed forward or back to change the four speeds. Braking was first class; unusually, the rear brake was operated by the heel of the right foot, the front conventionally from the right-hand lever. The headlamp assembly was incorporated within the handlebar which meant the beam always followed the direction of travel. Strangely, later models dropped this good idea, returning the assembly to the front legshield, whilst other manufacturers followed

the Diana's lead by siting theirs on the handlebar!

A possibly annoying feature of the Diana's design was that the main lighting switch was integral with the key-operated electric starter, situated just forward of the seat, which meant some fumbling in the dark when lights were required with the scooter in motion. Two six volt batteries were used in series for the electrics and these were situated below the rear seat, actually in a compartment in the top of the fuel tank. Chromium plating was used in several places on the machine, including flashes down both side panels, giving the model a very smart appearance. The fuel filler cap was locked away behind the front saddle, below which were the fusebox (not fitted on earlier models), and a small compartment where tools could be kept. The ignition contact breakers and dynastart brushgear, which, in those days, often required adjustment or cleaning, were easily accessible once a light aluminium cover was removed on the left side of the engine. For an engine with a dynastart this was a brilliant feature, as flywheel removal on virtually all other scooters with a similar facility meant special tools were necessary.

The Durkopp Company in Bielefeld, Germany was founded in 1867, producing bicycles and sewing machines and also light motorcycles using the Diana name; there was even a Diana car and a lorry at one time. In 1953 the Diana Scooter was first produced – one of the earliest in the postwar boom years – yet it was a well-researched and developed machine that found many buyers throughout Europe, in spite of its high price. It was a bestseller and deservedly so with good engine performance from its two-stroke engine, and a comfortable ride from a well-damped, coil sprung suspension system. Ten inch split rim wheels were used and adequate space was available below

*A Durkopp Diana standard (left) and Vespa 180.*

the rear carrier for a spare wheel. A large glovebox, which was lockable, was fitted behind the legshields. Many attractive accessories were available, including an unusual child's seat which could be mounted on the footboard between the rider's legs. Chromium-plated legshield side crash bars were an attractive extra, as were handlebar end-fitting rear view mirrors. The first engines were 175cc equipped with Bing carburettor and a very unusual, horizontally-inclined throttle slide, but soon a 194cc version producing 9.5hp replaced this.

The front suspension was one-sided initially, and was soon replaced by a double support, accompanied by a change in the shape of the front mudguard. The fuel tank was large, giving the machine a range of about 300km. The first Dianas were imported into the UK in 1956, selling for £214, which was expensive when compared to the Lambretta LD at £150, Vespa GS at £188, and Dayton at £198.

In 1959 a special, high performance 12hp model with dualseat and conventional rear footbrake was produced and named the Diana Sport. This sold for just £6 more than the standard model. The Sport was available in one colour only – flame red – and was a superb-looking machine, rivalling – at least to my mind – the timeless elegance and performance of the legendary Vespa GS. To permit better cooling of the

higher compression engine, the hot air exhaust was taken straight out through the left-hand side panel, via a circular grille, which turned out to have the additional benefit of warming the driver's left hand in colder weather! By 1960 a revised, heavier-looking front body shape was introduced, and the model was known as the TS, not an improvement, as far as I am concerned. The Diana Sport was still available but its unique body colour went and, with it, its mystique, as it then looked like any other Diana of the time.

Factory production ceased in Germany toward the end of 1961 after around 31,000 machines had been produced, and Durkopp moved on to production of industrial machinery. Sales of new Dianas in the UK continued up until early 1963, when there was still a waiting list of prospective customers.

### Heinkel Tourist

Ernst Heinkel's company, situated in Stuttgart, Germany, began producing motor scooters in July 1953.

The design was more upmarket than that of the Italian Vespas and Lambrettas, which were selling well. Heinkel chose a four-stroke engine for greater reliability with ease of refuelling. The suspension system did not dip on braking, giving the machine a much more stable feel on the road. The dualseat was also large and comfortable.

These were all advantageous features and the Tourist was so successful that it outsold all of the other makes in its home country. The first UK examples sold were rebadged as Excelsior by the importer, because it was felt that the Heinkel name would revive memories of the wartime bomber of the same name. However, the scooter did soon carry its proper moniker when it was seen that UK buyers did not havve a problem with the Messerschmitt bubblecar.

Due to an unfortunate UK pricing policy, the scooter was the most expensive available at that time, so sales were not large. Those who did purchase one were usually very satisfied with their choice, however, and, today, of

*A 1959 Durkopp Diana at Crich tramway museum in Derbyshire.*

... all the features
you've always
wanted—and never
found before

## that's luxury with a *Diana*

The Diana Scooter is built to perfection and *for* perfection—that is what makes it such an enthralling machine to ride. Press the starter button and the 200 c.c. engine purrs immediately into life, giving ample power with absolute safety because of the Diana's inherent road holding qualities. Comfort on the worst surfaces, phenomenal ease of handling in heavy traffic, an easy 50 m.p.h. at 95 m.p.g. with two up, and astonishing silence characterise this outstanding Scooter whilst its superb finish makes it a joy to own. Start now with a Diana—£218/6/3 inc. P.T. and worth every penny of its price—Alternatively, if you want a Moped, for £85/1/3 inc. P.T. there is the 48 c.c. *Dianette*

those makes imported to the UK, a larger proportion of Heinkels survive. Heinkel awarded medals to owners who covered large mileages on their scooters – very good publicity that inspired owner confidence – which have become collector's items today.

The prototype scooters were fitted with side panels, and a movable front mudguard similar to that of the Lambretta LD scooter. However, when the first commercial model, the A0, reached the streets, it had a very distinctive fixed triangular front. The solid body was completely and easily removable. It had a 150cc engine with a twist grip gearchange. The electrics were 6 volt, there was a kickstarter, and the wheels had 8 inch split rims.

In July 1954, the 102 A1 introduced a larger, 175cc engine, 12 volt electrics, and an electric dynaststarter system. The kickstarter was removed;

... and Clifton College, Bristol.

A 1962 Heinkel Tourist A2 at Budleigh Salterton in south Devon ...

# HEINKEL
## *Tourist*

only an electric starter was fitted but, unlike other makes, this was totally reliable.

In August 1955, the 103 A0 brought in a four-speed gearbox and ten inch wheels. The 103 A1 was introduced in September 1957 with a slightly more powerful engine, which was mounted on rubber bushes. The handlebars were faired-in, improving the appearance. The 103 A2, introduced in August 1969, had a more modern body style fitted with flashing direction indicators. The silencer was usefully coated by an anti-corrosion lacquer which gave it a very long life.

The Heinkel Cabin Cruiser bubblecar, by the way, used the 175cc scooter engine initially when introduced in October 1956. Engine capacity was later increased to 200cc. The model continued in production in various countries for ten years. A British-made version was known as the Trojan.

The Heinkel Tourist scooter had one of the longest production runs in the industry, and only Lambretta and Vespa models survived in the UK market when the last Tourist left the production line in December 1965. The Tourist is a large, well-built, heavy machine with excellent riding qualities, and is one of the most comfortable scooters to ride. Its reliability is legendary and, even today, is ridden by enthusiasts on long-distance rallies. Its main drawback was a less-than-ideal gearchange system which, strangely, was still no better at the end of the production run. Today, it is possible to purchase a foot gearchange modification for the Heinkel which overcomes the original problem.

Total production was around 170,000 scooters. In Germany, where a surprisingly large number of Heinkels have survived, there is a thriving owner's club and spares production industry.

## James

The history of the British classic scooter is a combination of some very good ideas tempered by conservatism, hesitation and lack of vision, especially in the styling department. So often, it was too little, too late ... The big names in British motorcycling were slower to join the market than were the new scooter companies. When they did eventually appear, their products showed promise but this, sadly, was not capitalised on.

James was an established motorcycle company known for its basic but reliable ride-to-work machines. When, at last in 1960, the company decided to produce a scooter, an appropriate name

A James SC1 scooter colour co-ordinates with a barge on Gloucestershire canal.

could not be thought of other than the James SC1, which doesn't call for a lot of imagination!

The origin of the SC1 came from an adaptation of the James Cadet engine where the cylinder was horizontal rather than vertical. An interesting and fresh idea was to locate the engine under the scooter footboard rather than conventionally under the seat. This freed up most of that area for useful storage, as well as giving the scooter a low centre of gravity, and thus excellent road-riding capability. At the end of a journey the rider could lock away his crash helmet rather than having to carry it around, a very useful facility and revolutionary at the time. (The Japanese reinvented the idea in the 1980s and made a huge success of it.)

The SC1 had a three-speed gearbox, with the battery and fuel tank situated under the seat, which still left enough space to carry shopping. The engine relied on natural, unassisted air flow for cooling. A large mudflap fitted behind the front wheel dealt with the prospective problem of water spray affecting the electrics for the sparkplug, which was situated in the

front of the engine. One odd feature was that cable controls for the carburettor had to pass over the top of the footboard, down through a rubber grommet and the footboard to the carburettor beneath. This, and the tickler rod, were sited right beside the rider's foot. A quickly removable centre panel gave access to the top of the engine.

The front suspension was leading fork, and twelve inch wheels were fitted. There were removable panels each side of the rear wheel to assist in access to it and the open drive chain. Ground clearance was low but this, in practice, was of little importance on normal roads. The frame of the James was a substantial tube that also ran around the sides of the legshields and, as such, it was a scooter well capable of supporting a more powerful engine than its 150cc two-stroke. However, the only development was that the SC2 received a four-speed gearbox in 1963.

*A 1960 James scooter beside an Austin lorry of the same period.*

# THE James

## 150 SCOOTER

*The Safest motor scooter*

The large, circular headlamp was mounted quite stylishly on the handlebars, ensuring that corners and bends were illuminated as the scooter went around them. Gear changing was via the traditional British system of a front right-hand foot pedal for changing up, and rear right-hand foot pedal for changing down. On the other side was the rear brake pedal. Styling was rather an acquired taste; rather bulky and substantial – but likeable.

Riding the James was a rewarding experience as it had good braking, balance and roadholding; the only thing lacking was a little more power. It appeared on the market at a sensible mid-range price of £165, and became even cheaper year-by-year until it ceased production in 1966. It was a good scooter and some examples managed to find an overseas market. There is evidence that some were sold in the USA under the Matchless brand name, no doubt hoping to cash in on the reputation of a much larger and well-known British motorcycle from within the same Associated Motorcycle Group of Companies.

A Lambretta TV175 series 2 (left) parked beside a series 1.

## Lambretta TV 175 series 2

In terms of the number of scooters sold in the UK, one name is better known than the rest: Lambretta. Its scooters may not have been the best (although many believe they were), but its publicity and marketing, aftersales service and ability to produce machines that appealed to the majority certainly were.

Lambretta's success in the UK was due, to a large extent, to the British importer Lambretta Concessionaires of Croydon, which set up the best service centres for any scooter throughout the UK, backed up by excellent spares and accessories availability. In virtually every other country, Vespa was the bestseller, but in the UK Lambretta was King and Britain became its largest market outside of Italy.

To some extent at the beginning of scooter production in 1947, Lambretta followed Vespa in everything that company did, although was slow to replicate the idea of enclosing the mechanicals. Lambrettas were popular, but it wasn't until they acquired bodywork and chic styling that sales really took off.

The first good seller was the model LD, first produced in 1953 and the first scooter designed to have bodywork, as the earlier LC was essentially an open scooter modified to accept bodywork. Lambrettas did start life with fully enclosed shaft drive, a great improvement on the open chains of conventional motorcycles and a feature which set

A Lambretta TV175 near Birnbeck Pier, Weston-super-Mare in Somerset.

GET AROUND BETTER—*TRAVEL* **Lambretta**

THE WORLD'S FINEST SCOOTER

them apart and attracted many buyers. No fewer than 53,000 Mk1 125cc LDs were produced by the Italian Innocenti Company in Milan, located beside the river Lambrate (hence the Lambretta name). This is an incredible figure, that one model exceeding the total production run of several other scooter makes throughout their lifespans. Total production of all the various variations of the LD model was in the region of 400,000 units, which does illustrate just how big the desire for scooters was in the mid-1950s. Eventually, to meet demand, Lambrettas were made under licence in several other countries, including South America.

The buying public was demanding more power in its scooters, especially in the UK, as illustrated by the popularity of the sporty Vespa GS model. So, in 1957, Lambretta produced a completely new scooter model called the TV 175, the initials standing for 'touring at high velocity'. This was bigger, more streamlined and more stable. The engine, gearbox and drive were housed in a horizontal unit slung low in the frame. Sadly, gone was the shaft drive due to high production costs but, in its place, was a parallel two-chain drive running in an enclosed oil bath.

In 1958 the Li series appeared; essentially, new 125cc and 150cc engines in a TV-style body. Sales of these machines really took off and no fewer than 475,000 examples were produced by Innocenti. The Li had exactly the right combination of style, performance reliability and price that the majority of buyers were looking for.

In 1959 the TV series 2 was produced based on a higher performance version of the Li engine rather than the original TV engine which was discontinued. Both the Li and TV models had their headlamps repositioned on the handlebars from the legshields to improve lighting when going around corners and bends.

The TV series 2 became the success the series 1 had hoped to be, accepted as the best Lambretta ever to date. Sales were 30 per cent higher than for the series 1.

The TV series 2 resembles the Li series 2, but closer inspection reveals twin shock absorbers on the modified front suspension, and a speedometer top speed of 70mph rather than 50mph. Chromium-plated TV 175 badges are fitted to the sidepanels, and a dualseat was standard. The electrics were improved and a stronger headlamp fitted.

In later years slimmer bodywork was produced, known as the Slimline series. 200cc engines appeared

but without the distinctive TV initials which robbed them of some of their mystique.

The scooter had its faults, of course, like any other, and the most annoying was that the kickstarter required a lot of effort, even then producing only a few revolutions of the engine. The kickstart was small and its degree of travel meant that the bike had to be leant away from the rider to prevent pounding the pedal into the ground. Starting a TV in front of passers-by could be a very embarrassing experience if it wasn't set up correctly. The ignition key was mounted horizontally and, when worn, could vibrate out of the keyhole and fall away, the engine continuing to run.

Lambrettas were manufactured in Italy until 1971 when a protracted strike forced the firm to sell out to British Leyland for car production, by which time around two-and-a-half million Lambretta scooters had been produced.

Today, this Lambretta is one of the easiest scooters to restore because so many parts have been remanufactured by a large range of specialist dealers.

## Lambretta Vega

By 1968 the scooter market had become a shadow of its former self, with all manufacturers save Lambretta and Vespa gone to the wall. The scooter buyer's choice was limited to a machine from one of these two, therefore, which did help sustain sales levels for a while. Just ten years earlier customers could have selected from around fifty different manufacturers, most of whom offered several different models.

Lambretta still had the lion's share of the market, due largely to the fact that there were over a thousand officially appointed dealers, and the many Lambretta owner's clubs still active throughout the country.

It was with justified pride that in November 1968 Mr A James Agg, Managing Director Of Lambretta Concessionaires Ltd, announced the launch of a new range of scooters, collectively known as The Luna Line (known as Lui in Italy). The new models were styled by the famous Italian designer Bertone, who had the designs of many exotic sports cars to his credit. Lambretta intended that these machines would resurrect the scooter's mass popularity, and were described as having "... the year 2000 look".

The launch took place at the London Planetarium in front of the trade and motoring press. Present also were representatives from the Royal Aircraft Establishment of Farnborough, which had supplied £10,000 worth of space research equipment for

A futuristic-looking Lambretta Vega by a modern office building in Bristol ...

... and keeping company with a period Royal Blue coach in Swindon in Wiltshire.

display use at the launch. Described as a revolutionary breakaway from traditional design, the scooters were compact and lightweight, with futuristic styling. They were simple, and could be easily worked on with engines – newly-designed, fuel efficient two-strokes of low capacity – in the open.

Three models were produced: the three-speed, 50cc Luna (which was not imported to the UK); the four-speed, 75cc Vega, and the four-speed 75cc Cometa. The Cometa was fitted with a separate crankcase oil injection system which did away with the hassle of mixing oil with petrol when filling up. It was also claimed to produce more efficient combustion, more power, and have lower running costs.

Prices were £130 for the Vega and £149 for the Cometa, which included a 30 per cent purchase tax imposed by the UK government, so they were very good value for money and affordable to many. Innocenti Lambretta had managed to cut production costs to a minimum. Dealers made a profit of £20 per machine. Futuristic names were chosen for the various colour schemes, including Orbit Orange, Martian Red, and Luna Dust!

It is interesting to read the text of Mr Agg's speech, in which he speculates about the kind of lives we might be living in the year 2000. It seems that, when not riding scooters, we would all be regular space travellers in our very own private space ships ...

Because of its small size, Lambretta claimed that fifteen Vegas could be parked in one car parking space, thus solving overcrowding in urban streets. Being narrower, lighter, and more manoeuvrable than any other two-wheeler, the company claimed the Vega was ideal for every member of the family; suitable for commuting, shopping, sporting events and long-distance travel, yet offering complete comfort, safety, and minimal purchase and running costs.

In fact, Lambretta had returned to an earlier design approach of the 1950s, whereby the engine

THREE SPACE-AGE MODELS

THE LAMBRETTA « LUNA 50 »
The ideal commuter transport for all the family wanting an economical vehicle for work or popping down to the shops — flexible three speed gearbox means very little gear changing in traffic, low tax and insurance, over 170 miles on one gallon of petrol, cruises comfortably and makes « Luna » a must for every one who has ever bought a bus ticket.

THE LAMBRETTA « VEGA 75 » AND « COMETA 75 »
Countdown through the gears. First - second - third - fourth now you and the girl friend are gliding down a country lane on your way to the sea at a cruising speed of well over 50 m.p.h. Just the job for the sporty would-be astronaut type who wants that extra surge of powerful acceleration. The « Vega » and « Cometa », both have sparkling performances — top speed 60 m.p.h. — 130 miles per gallon — low tank and insurance. The vital difference is however in the lubrication system. The « Vega 75 » operates on a standard petrol/oil mixture of 2 % whereas the « Cometa 75 » has the space-age sophistication of an oil injection system which operates automatically from two separate tanks one pure petrol - one pure oil.

Common dimensions: 65 ½"; width and handlebars 26" height 42 ½" seat height 31 ½"; wheelbase 47 ½.
LAMBRETTA CONCESSIONAIRES LTD. Lambretta House, Purley Way, Croydon, Surrey.

INNOCENTI

SOC. GENERALE PER L'INDUSTRIA METALLURGICA E MECCANICA
MILANO   ROMA   NEW YORK   PARIS   LONDON   CARACAS   DÜSSELDORF

Marketing Pubblicita Generale 2/v/

was exposed but the rider was provided with weather protection. The scooters were individual in appearance, with good mechanical simplicity and accessibility. They really were economic, light and very reliable and would be perfectly acceptable today as a contemporary design. Perhaps 'today' would have provided their best market; back in 1968, sales were not as good as had been hoped for, even though the machines were advanced in design and very good value for money.

The engines were good, admittedly, and, even today, these machines can be seen in scooter sporting and racing events, but in 1968, riders – at least in the UK – were used to, liked and preferred scooters with larger, fully-enclosed engines. Some markets received their Luna Line Scooters fitted with flashing direction indicators, though not the UK, perhaps in an effort to keep ticket price to an absolute minimum.

There was a small range of special accessories, including a luggage carrier and fold-up foot pegs for a pillion rider. The so-called dualseat was a misnomer as it was not long enough to *safely* seat two people. There was a steering lock for security but no ignition key.

The Lubematic system on the Cometa was a crankcase oil injection arrangement, a step into the future which is today taken for granted. Current sales figures proved, however, that the buying public preferred the cheaper, manual fuel-mixing Vega, which just goes to show that it takes time for new ideas to be appreciated and become accepted. Production of the scooters continued for only eighteen months or so.

Around 35,000 Luna Line scooters were produced in total, a tenth of the sales achieved by Lambretta's bestseller, the Li series, ten years previously and forty years before the year 2000.

Shortly afterward Lambretta – perhaps the greatest name in UK scootering – ceased to exist, after suffering a long industrial dispute. Innocenti converted the factory to produce its version of some British Leyland cars and scooter production facilities were sold to India. It was the end of an era.

## Maicoletta

In 1956 at the age of sixteen, I had no real knowledge of motor scooters other than

that I liked them. I was not impressed by conventional motorcycles; those I had come across seemed noisy, dirty, and uncivilised. Scooters, by comparison, were smart, quiet, comfortable, user-friendly and stylish: very attractive! I knew nothing about little wheels, top speeds, or riding in wet or slippery conditions. I found I liked the kind of people who rode scooters. They wore normal clothes, you could see their faces, and they seemed more civilised than the rough, begoggled, black-booted, strap-laden motorcyclists I had come across.

My parents knew even less than me about scooters which, after all, had only been on the roads for a year or so. They faintly disapproved of them because they were mostly foreign-made, and by their arch enemies in the war they had lived through. Still, they were just about to push their

A Maico Maicoletta poses with a period steam railway crane at the east Somerset railway at Cranmore.

Taking it easy in a garden in Bristol.

# MAICOLETTA

## The most powerful German Motor Scooter

### 175 + 250 cc

only son out into the big, wide world to live away from home and begin an apprenticeship, and he needed some cheap transport to be able to get around. At least scooters – with their legshields, footboard, enclosed engine and large windscreen – would keep him drier than would a motorcycle.

My father thought – perhaps with good reason – that as the best motorcycles were British-made, it must be right that a British-made scooter would be best. So along came a Piatti which, though it had an Italian-sounding name, was made in Byfleet in Surrey. The Piatti was cheaper than a Vespa, there was a dealer close to where I lived, and I quite liked the look of it. I wasn't interested in going fast, preferring comfort, style and good weather protection. The brochure said it would do 45mph which I thought fast enough. In practice, however, 38mph was more like it, meaning my regular, 130 mile journeys could take rather a long time to complete ...

As my first scooter, although very much loved, was not really up to the job I needed it for, after about a year I made up my mind to try and acquire a much larger, faster scooter; something with larger wheels. I was an avid reader of all the new scooter magazines and I really liked what I had read about the German Maicoletta which received many good reviews and had won many awards in sporting activities.

One weekend whilst visiting my parents, I rode the Piatti into town and had a look at a second-hand Maicoletta in a motorcycle dealer's showroom. The dealer said I could take it out for a test drive, something I had no knowledge of. I thought the scooter was great, just what I needed, and must have been out on it for an hour or more. I took it home to show my parents, who would have to put up most of the money. However, they were not at all impressed by it, and flatly told me no. I was not at all popular with the dealer when I eventually took the scooter back!

The Maicoletta has a certain magic about it, being really big, stable and powerful (I didn't see why scooters had to suffer little wheels or little engines). It was first produced in Germany in 1955 by an established motorcycle company which had already made a very advanced machine called a Maicomobile. This offered all the weather protection of a scooter, plus large wheels and built-in storage lockers. It didn't have a flat footboard, however, as it really was an enclosed motorcycle. The Maicoletta, on the other hand, had a perfectly flat footboard and a large comfortable dualseat and a larger engine of

250cc: there was even a 277cc version. A smaller, 175cc engine was offered on the German market. It was well appointed, complete with wind-up mechanical clock on the dashboard and gear-selected indicator, which was useful. The body could be quickly and easily removed in order to work on the engine.

It did have one serious drawback, however, and that was a relatively unreliable electric starter system, fed from a six volt battery supply, nor was there a kickstart. The starter was of a strange design which entailed the engine being rocked backward and forward, faster and faster, until it ran past top dead centre and – hopefully – started, though very often it just kept rocking without starting, which simply flattened the small battery. It was a heavy machine to push-start! When I restored mine that problem prevailed, but other people I have spoken to about this have devised all sorts of set-up procedures for the electric contact breakers which they claim overcome the problem.

The Maicoletta was always expensive to buy but demand continued, despite this. Incredibly, the importer continued to satisfy that demand for some years after production ceased in 1962 by making complete machines from its extensive stocks of spare parts!

## Manurhin Hobby

From the front, the Hobby looks rather more like a motorcycle than a scooter initially, because of its large, spoked sixteen inch wheels, and many scooterists, back in the 1950s and '60s dismissed it out of hand as not a 'proper' scooter. This was a pity as there's no getting away from the fact that larger wheels do give better roadholding, but as style, rather than mechanical attributes, were uppermost in most scooterists' minds at the time, UK sales of the Hobby were disappointing.

This aside, the Hobby was a big step forward in scooter design, setting the trend in automatic scooters which now is almost universal. It was originally designed by the German firm DKW, and first produced in 1954. Not only was gear changing simplified but starting was made easier by the fitting of a hand pullcord, as in modern lawnmowers. That idea did not catch on, and at times I've wondered why; certainly, ladies wearing delicate footwear would have found it easier.

The Hobby sold well in Germany and proved itself a sturdy, reliable machine. The engine, though

rear body would pivot up from the rear, giving good access to the engine, and a door at the front allowed access to the fuel tap and carburettor. The footboard was perfectly flat and the legshield came up high for good protection from the weather and road dirt. Frontal styling was an acquired taste, as previously mentioned, and didn't match the rest of the machine, which had lines that were smooth and clean. The Hobby's large diameter drum brakes were good in operation.

Another departure from standard scooter design was that the stand folded out from the side of the footboard and the scooter simply leant on it; no effort was needed to pull it onto its stand. As soon as the machine was lifted off the stand a return spring folded it back into position.

The late 1950s was a time of great expansion for German factories and in 1957 production of the Hobby was transferred to a new factory near the River Rhine in France.

DKW stopped Hobby production in 1958, and expanded its work on cars as part of the AutoUnion group.

At the new French factory scooters identical to the original DKW Hobby were produced initially, but gradually improvements were made. The clutch became fully automatic and the chain drive fully enclosed. Two seats were fitted as standard and the passenger's feet were now able to rest on rearward extensions of the footboards. Wider tyres were fitted and more power obtained from the engine by fitting a French Gurtner carburettor in place of the original German Bing.

Continental sales were good, but in the UK Italian designs ruled the roost: buyers were put off by those spoked, sixteen inch wheels! When Triumph brought out its automatic Tina, with its little disc wheels, a few years later, it sold in much greater numbers!

*Above & opposite: One of the last-produced Manurhin Hobbys.*

only 75cc and well silenced, still managed to keep up with town traffic. There was still a clutch to engage the drive but from there on gear changing was automatic. The belt system with variable diameter pulley drive is still used today. The whole of the

Roller
„Kleider machen Leute"
ganz besonders heute!

...aber merke und notiere:
Hobby fahren Kavaliere..

...lten – nur fahren! DKW
Hobby

SCOOTER
MANURHIN

The only Scooter
in the World with an
entirely automatic transmission

Beltamatic
Integral

**Simplicity in starting.
Simplicity in driving.**

Thanks to this remarkable feature, the Manurhin scooter is controlled as easily and simply as a modern automobile with an automatic transmission.

The three horse-power motor can easily handle two people on any road — on the level, or in the mountains. The "Variator" always selects the proper ratio between motor and rear wheel speed to give maximum performance under changing conditions.

The speed (limited purposely to 40 m.p.h.) coupled with the 16 in. wheels, the front telescopic fork and rear swinging arm suspension, combine to give this machine the comfort, safety, stability and ease of operation, which every one has been seeking.

The price is within reach of every one.

The MANURHIN is not only an evolution, it is a REVOLUTION.

In November 1960 the importer decided to give the Hobby a new image by renaming it the Manurhin Concorde! (The name Manurhin is derived from Manufactured by the River Rhine.) Sales did not improve, however, and part of the remaining stock was sold off at discount prices, although some remained unsold many years after production ceased.

## Moby SV 125

When I became interested in scooters the first time around in the fifties, I remember seeing a few Lambrettas on the road that didn't look quite right – the model Ds. They didn't have an enclosed body and, to me, they were not proper scooters – machines that should cover over the oily bits and look stylish! However, what I didn't realise then was that these were cheaper to produce and so could be sold for less. They did appeal to those who liked to tinker with the mechanics, which were easier to get at.

Motobecane, the French scooter manufacturer, looked at the Lambretta D and a few other similar Italian machines, and decided that there was a significant market in its own country for such a scooter. Previously, Motobecane had produced an upmarket four-stroke scooter as early as 1951, and in 1954, produced the 'Utilitaire' SV using a two-stroke, 125cc engine. The Lambretta design had been closely followed, but this model had a simpler, cheaper, enclosed rear drive chain, rather than a shaft drive. The suspension was very simple, and used a circular rubber bung at the rear and concentric rubber bands at the front.

The Utilitaire was basic and cheap but quite effective in operation, and had the added benefit of being relatively lightweight, thus maximising engine performance. Only one saddle was fitted, again to reduce cost and weight. Below this was a useful large glovebox running the whole length of the left-hand side of the scooter. Mirroring it on the other side was the fuel tank. On top of both behind the saddle was a useful carrier.

The spare wheel was fitted to the rear and the registration plate and rear light enclosed within and over it. Weather protection stopped at knee height, but did give protection from road surface water blown back from the front wheel. A mudflap was fitted to

*A Moby Utilitaire with Burgh Island, south Devon, in the background.*

A Moby 150 near County Gate on Exmoor, West Somerset.

the rear of the front mudguard. Over the front wheel was another carrier. The headlamp turned with the handlebars so the rider could actually see where he was going. The engine flywheel had some fan blades attached, and a small cover forced air up over the cylinder which, being uncovered, was open to natural airflow anyway. Overall, this was a simple, efficient, cheap and practical design which sold well in its native country.

In the UK we had become used to identical models carrying different badges, such as BSA and Triumph, and in France it was the same with Motobecane and Motoconfort. The brand name for both versions was Moby.

The wheels were 10 inch split rims. The 3-speed gearbox was operated by a handlebar twistgrip, which allowed the machine to attain a top speed of 50mph with 40mph a more practical level to maintain.

The SV175 continued to sell until 1957, when it was developed into a full-bodied version with removable side panels and full height legshields known as the SVH. This had two saddles and the speedometer incorporated into the rear of the headlamp, and was available in the UK, unlike its predecessor. The SVH continued until 1960, when – like a lot of other companies worldwide – Motobecane left the scooter market altogether to concentrate on Mobylette mopeds, which achieved vast sales in France and also sold very well in other European countries, including the UK.

Raleigh eventually took over the rights to the Mobylette and manufactured it in this country. Raleigh later made the Bianchi Bear Cub scooter under licence from Italy, calling it the Raleigh Roma – but that's another story!

## Piatti

It's been said that no-one ever forgets their first scooter, and this certainly is true for me. It wasn't a fast scooter, or a particularly reliable one, but what a great character it had! Neither Vespa nor Lambretta, I went for something different; more out of ignorance than inspiration, I chose a Piatti, as I liked its individual appearance, colour, light weight and low purchase price.

# Moby Scooter

BREVET S.G.D.G.
N° 667.318

*Pour les services les plus durs*

1956

## CARACTÉRISTIQUES

**Type S. B. "UTILITAIRE"** Bloc-moteur 2 temps - Cylindrée 125 cm³ - Mise en marche par kick starter - 3 vitesses au guidon - Cylindre aluminium chromé dur - Transmission inusable à chaîne sous carter étanche à bain d'huile - Suspension AV par anneaux Neiman, AR par evidgom Hutchinson - Grands porte-bagages AV et AR - Compteur de vitesse - Puissant éclairage AV et AR - Roues AV et AR interchangeables de grandes dimensions (3,5×10) - Larges repose-pieds pour le passager - Réservoir d'essence (7 litres) avec filtre a décantation - Garde-boue et tablier assurant une excellente protection - Châssis monobloc en tubes d'acier avec ensemble oscillant moteur-transmission - Deux freins très puissants tambours de 130 m/m - Poids 75 kgs - Vitesse en palier : 70 km h

103.000 Frs.

500 Francs

CRÉDIT

## Why YOU should buy a Moby scooter

- Lowest Price High Quality 150 c.c. Scooter
- Robust Tubular Construction, Attractive Two-Tone finish
- Spare wheel and pillion seat included

classic elegance and superb two-tone finish distinguish
Mobyscooter. Simplicity of design coupled with
robust construction ensure for the rider
nparalleled degree of safety and reliability.
erformance too is on the same high
level while economy is such
that the running costs
are negligible.

## Specification

le transfer single cylinder,
lined aluminium cylinder.

ary drive to gearbox; rear
losed.

with multiplate clutch con-
dlebar lever and twist grip.

neto, high tension, with

rame of electro-welded steel
cowl giving full protection.

section affording adequate
times.

nk with patented Neiman
Swinging Arm with Evigdon
shioning.

**Wheels:** Interchangeable, with balloon 3.5 × 10 tyres.

**Brakes:** Internal expanding hub brakes. Rear controlled by foot pedal; front by handlebar lever.

**Electrical Equipment:** 6-volt headlamp with dipping switch, rear lamp and horn.

**Speedometer:** Built into headlamp.

**Finish:** Attractively enamelled in cream/maroon. All bright parts chromium plated.

**Equipment:** Pillion seat, spare wheel. Comprehensive tool kit in large heavy duty steel container.

**Optional Extras:** Rear luggage carrier, chromium plated, £5. Front luggage carrier, stove enamelled, £2.5.0.

**Weight:** 216 lb.

**Speed:** Approximately 45/50 m.p.h.

**Fuel Consumption:** Approximately 80/90 m.p.g.

£139·19·0 (inc. P.Tax)
Complete with pillion seat and spare wheel

A Cyclemaster Piatti alongside a two-tone period Guy bus in Derbyshire.

A Piatti in motion at Filton Park, Bristol.

I was seventeen years old and, as previously mentioned, my first vehicle had not only to transport me and my luggage around town, but also on a regular 130 mile journey from Bristol, where I lodged and worked, to Plymouth where my parents still lived.

The little Piatti carried me on summer touring holidays and in the winter through snow and ice. Every now and then it would develop mechanical problems; on one epic journey in the dark, it blew its rear light bulb. Being a direct current system, this meant that the front light received more voltage and soon afterwards also blew. To make matters worse it began to snow. When I pulled over to stop, I found that the stand had frozen to the frame and would not descend: what a night!

A Belgian-built Piatti beside the tracks of the Romney Hythe and Dymchurch miniature railway in Kent.

The Piatti was under-developed, and several mechanical parts fractured as a result which was frustrating, inconvenient, and expensive. On the positive side it was great fun to ride, small, stable and manoeuvrable. The pressed steel monocoque bodywork was well made with a very good paint finish. It was available in several colours: red, black, blue, cream, and duotone.

It was designed by Vincent Piatti, an Italian engineer who had worked in various European countries including the UK. He foresaw the potential of the motor scooter in the very early 1950s when only Piaggio had the same idea with the Vespa. The Piatti scooter was developed in Italy but, surprisingly, never produced there. Piatti claimed that his inspiration for the model came from the British Corgi. An early prototype had the headlamp situated low down at the nose where the air intake is now; in motion it would have quickly overheated, as there was no front air intake, nor a cooling fan. First appearing at the Brussels Salon in 1952, production

**stable... par tous les temps**

**Piatti**

**125 cc**

**le scooter qui marque une étape décisive**

got under way in Belgium a couple of years later.

The D'Ieteren Company of Brussels was the first to produce the Piatti. It was available in a grey finish only (at that time, not many manufacturers offered a colour choice, anyway). Accurate information is difficult to come by regarding the number produced, as the original company is defunct. Those records that do exist seem to indicate that only around 800 of the initially proposed 5000 scooters were actually built.

Sales were difficult to achieve in Belgium at that time, due to much competition and the fact that the scooter boom and decline there was several years ahead of that in Britain. Production of the Piatti in Belgium ceased in 1957.

The Belgian Piatti did offer one of the most unusual scooter accessories ever; a wickerwork basket shaped to completely cover the front of the scooter, which fitted below the headlamp ahead of the legshields. It had a lift-up lid and was designed to hold parcels and shopping. A gap was provided for the air intake at the nose.

Cyclemaster began Piatti production in England in 1956. This company was well known at the time for its motorised rear pedal cycle wheel. The firm had a past association with Vincent Piatti in the design of add-on engines for conventional bicycles. After a bright start, however, sales declined as word of its unreliability spread.

On the road it was noticeable that the Piatti was much slower than similarly-priced machines from Vespa and Lambretta. This was a great pity as Cyclemaster was to be praised for its good advertising and establishment of a widespread service network, which, the advertising claimed, extended to 26 different countries.

At a time when most British manufacturers had adopted a 'wait and see' policy regarding scooter production, some British Piattis were exported to France, in the hope, perhaps, that they could satisfy a demand that had resulted when the Belgian version had disappeared.

A single seat version followed the original model, without a spare wheel, which permitted an even lower retail price. I didn't notice many on the roads, however.

On a practical level, widespread use of screws rather than bolts caused problems after heads became worn as many components could not be removed or tightened unless the engine was first removed from the body.

A mark two version of the Piatti was announced in late 1957 which overcame many of the original faults, such as overheating and dirt entering the carburettor and the gearchange mechanism. Sadly, few reached the sales rooms.

Of course, the Piatti did have good features, too. Locating the luggage carrier at the front made for good weight distribution; there wasn't a gap between windscreen and front legshields through which rain and wind could permeate; rear springing was adjustable, and the twistgrip gearchange was positive stop, so gear selections weren't missed. In addition, the steering could be locked by a simple padlock, and extra storage space was available within the dualseat and the spare wheel. Both seat and handlebars were adjustable for height to suit all riders. Then, too, the engine design – a low-slung, pivoted horizontal unit, and inline gearbox with a chain drive running in a sealed oilbath – was years ahead of Lambretta.

Not so clever was the notion that engine maintenance could be carried out by laying the scooter on its side, after closing a seal on the petroil cap. This was not a viable proposition when it was necessary to clear the sparkplug of a whisker in the rain in a busy street with a carrier full of luggage! (This was a common problem with the Piatti in spite of a specially-designed KLG plug with a rotating earth terminal.)

Sales of the British Piatti are thought to be around

Introducing

THE NEW 125cc. *Piatti*

The All-British Made Scooter

A CYCLEMASTER PRODUCT

15,000 scooters, more than three times that of the Belgian version.

Vincent Piatti is still active and lives in London. He is reported to have said that the Belgian model bought him a very nice car and the British a very nice house!

The Piatti was a machine of great character and innovation, in some ways years ahead of its time. Its downfall was insufficient development when many other great scooters were taking the market by storm.

Today, it is considered a milestone in motor scooter development. There are websites which proclaim its worth, and restored examples – of which there are not many – can be found on several continents.

A truly unique machine which deserves its place in history, Cyclemaster sales publicity material described it as "Sturdy as a young Lion, Light as a Feather, The Scooter for Tomorrow and All British" – well, almost!

## Puch Alpine

Steyr Daimler Puch of Austria was a well-established company which began making motor vehicles in 1901, and was one of the first companies outside of Italy to make motor scooters.

In 1952, Steyr Daimler Puch produced a 121cc, two-stroke machine known as the RL which had rod-operated gears. It was available only in a dull red colour and had 12 inch wheels.

In 1955 an electric starter (then a revolutionary idea) became available on the scooter which was called the RLA.

Puch scooters were rather sturdy machines, capable of heavy work; there was even a version with permanent sidecar for commercial use. The entire rear bodywork was hinged at the front and could be held open by a support to allow engine access.

In 1960 the Puch scooter was further improved visually with smoother lines, and also mechanically. It was given a model name rather than just a number, and engine size increased to 150cc. The headlamp was mounted higher towards the top of the legshields, and turned with the handlebars, which were faired-in.

The Puch Alpine sold very well in the UK and was imported by a firm called Ryders Autoservice of Liverpool. The local police force was persuaded to use them, which resulted in good national publicity, as usually only British-made motorcycles were purchased by a public body.

The engine produced 6.8bhp and was fitted with a three-speed gearbox controlled by cables from a twistgrip on the handlebars. Available colours were red and cream or blue and cream, and twin-tone blue later. A dualseat could be specified in place of twin seats.

The Puch came with two separate stands. The centre stand was very stable but required a lot of effort to get the machine on it. A side grab handle was intended to assist with this but most owners preferred to use the fold-out side stand, anyway, unless doing some work on the machine.

To illustrate our far simpler and trusting world then, a hand pump was fitted in full view within the legshields, although there was a lockable compartment for tools in the left-hand side panel. The six volt battery was housed in a similar compartment in the right-hand side panel, with space for two if an electric starter was fitted. The lighting remained as direct current, which was not ideal as the degree of brilliance depended on engine speed. The whole of the bodywork hinged forward to give access to the engine, and an opening panel on the left-hand side allowed operation of the fuel tap.

A rare version of the scooter, known as the Venus (no connection with the German scooter that went by the same name), had a foot-controlled gearchange.

The Alpine established itself as a fine rider's machine with good handling and brakes. A thriving owners club organised many sporting activities, and the Alpine was a familiar sight on our roads. In 1963 the importer decided to stop selling it in the UK, much to the dismay of the club. Members managed to effect a change of heart, however, and imports began again the next year at the original selling price of around £170. Sales were good until 1966, when production ceased, due largely to Europe-wide competition from the little Japanese step-through machines which brought about the demise of the ailing scooter market

## Raleigh Roma

In 1960 the UK scooter boom was at its peak and many established British companies decided to get in on the act. Raleigh Industries of Nottingham, doing well producing the French Mobylette moped under license, contacted the Italian Bianchi Company and arranged to produce its Orsetto (which means bear cub) scooter in the UK. It was decided to rename the machine the Raleigh Roma for the UK, giving it an Italian association (even though it was made in Nottingham and not Rome!).

A Puch Alpine scooter receives admiring looks at Bristol Zoo ...

# SR-SRA 150
## ALPINE MODEL

SRA 150

**PUCH**

CONCESSIONAIRES FOR GREAT BRITAIN
**RYDERS AUTOSERVICE** 215 KNOWSLEY ROAD LIVERPOOL 20

*... and is captured on film by David Sparrow.*

**SR SRA**

*...mit nur guten Seiten*

In some ways the Roma emulated the Piatti design: the horizontal engine was ram air-cooled with an in-line gearbox, and situated low between the wheels for good stability. Engine access was much easier, however, as a panel could be very easily removed from on top of the engine. On both sides the footboards hinged outward, clear all of mechanical components.

The 78cc, two-stroke engine produced 3.7bhp, and the three gears were selected by handlebar twistgrip. Plastic was used for some parts – such as the chain guard – although original use of that material for the footboards was discontinued. All panels were rubber-edged to avoid metal-to-metal contact. A useful storage area under the dualseat was not quite large enough to store a crash helmet. An air scoop fitted on top of the front mudguard was designed to improve cooling airflow over the engine. A good idea was the facility of forward and back adjustment of the dualseat to suit individual riders.

In 1962 an improved version was produced with slightly increased power output of 4.3bhp, different gear ratios, and revised exhaust system, now situated completely out of sight below the left-hand footboard. The little 8 inch wheels were fitted with 5 inch brakes

that were very efficient, and the shock absorbers – which appeared conventional – were actually filled with rubber. The Roma was available in a cream colour only (strangely, called pearl grey). Sales were good, and some examples were exported and seen at foreign shows.

In 1961 and '62, factory riding teams were entered in the prodigious Isle of Man Scooter Rally and won awards in the 24 hour endurance event, an especially worthy accomplishment for a low capacity machine.

An unusual feature of the Roma was its fuel cap, essentially just a plastic bung that was pushed into a hole in the top of the fuel tank under the seat. The little wheels made the scooter very manoeuvrable and easy to push around, and it became a very popular scooter for lady riders as a result. It sold for £117 with an unbelievably low annual road tax of just £1 because of its small engine capacity. The purchase price later fell to £95 and the Roma became a common sight on Britain's roads.

At the end of 1964 Bianchi decided to stop producing the Orsetto as sales were dropping. Parts for the Roma dried up and the little scooter ceased production. Raleigh went into decline as moped sales

A Raleigh Roma close to Burgh Island, south Devon ...

**RIGHT** in front for performance, economy and dependability. **RIGHT** in style with pearl grey enamel finish and chromium plated fittings. **RIGHT** on price-less than you'd think possible! SEE THE *RALEIGH*

# ROMA
### AT YOUR DEALERS RIGHT AWAY!

also fell and soon another great British company bit the dust.

The Roma had enjoyed a certain charm and was well developed: it was sad to see it go.

## Servetta Royspeed

When Lambretta scooter production ceased in Italy in 1971, that was not the end of the story, as European production of a Spanish variant of the Lambretta continued there. The company concerned was called Servetta and the scooters it produced were similar to the Italian Lambretta GP model, albeit with some styling differences and in the location of ignition and lighting switches and the storage compartment.

Amongst enthusiasts there was the feeling that this was not a true Lambretta, nor were the engines

as powerful or as reliable as the Italian-made Lambretta. As supplies of the original Lambretta items dried up, the need increased to tune-up the Spanish engines in order to improve performance. There were also those who wanted to do the same with their original Lambrettas.

A UK company that specialised in this field was Roys of Hornchurch, based in Essex. Its strategy was to offer bolt-on parts that the average owner could fit to his scooter to instantly improve performance without the need for specialist tuning equipment. The idea worked well and the firm was very quick to ensure that its name was visible on the

*. . . and in a Bristol park.*

A Servetta Royspeed at Filton, Bristol as Concorde passes overhead ...

modified machines, so increasing public awareness of its products. Roys also sold specially subsidised and painted side panels for Lambrettas bearing the name Royspeed in bold graphics, which the owner proudly showed off as something special: very good for business! This service was restricted to Lambrettas and Servettas, for which significant performance improvements could be made.

In any case, Vespa engines were very well developed at the Piaggio factory. Piaggio had seen its closest rival fail and was eager to maintain existing, and acquire new, business, so continuous development was the name of the game.

Deliveries from the Spanish factory were very erratic and unreliable, so, quite often, Roys was the best source of a new machine. Royspeed also offered special price discounts to buyers who were scooter club members, and some batches of Servettas were modified by Royspeed direct from the factory before sale to the public.

Besides improved carburettor and exhaust systems, Roys marketed more complex components such as stronger clutches and five-speed gearboxes. The latter resulted in great improvement in acceleration and were reliably designed and reasonably priced. For example, £29 for a five-speed gearbox seems unbelievable today, even allowing for inflation.

Larger cylinders and pistons were also available. Roys' modified lightweight Vega scooters were particularly successful in competition, and some can still be seen at events today.

Royspeed began its bolt-on tuning business in 1967, and amassed years of experience in competitive events on its fleet of test Lambrettas before making the fully developed tune-up parts

90

*...now keeping company with a Lambretta TV175 in a garden in Bristol.*

available to the general public. The brightly painted Royspeed service vans were very visible at performance sporting events, including the prestigious Isle of Man Scooter Rally. Successfully balancing performance, reliability and reasonable cost gained the company an enviable reputation, underlined by the fact that it cared about its customers and the work it did.

Royspeed – best remembered for its reputation and giving the scooter enthusiast what he wanted – survived well into the 1980s, whilst rival companies came and went.

### Triumph Tina & T10

About two years after the Tigress scooter appeared on the market, Triumph decided to produce a smaller machine of low capacity that would be lighter and much easier to ride, something of particular appeal to the ladies. It would have an automatic gearchange, very simple controls, and retail at less than £100. In theory, the proposition was a good one for which there should have been a large and ready market. There was then only one other automatic scooter on

the UK market, the Manurhin from France, which was a development of the earlier German DKW Hobby. It did have a much higher price tag, and large, spoked type wheels which were a turn-off for most scooter buyers.

The Tina incorporated several good ideas such as bolt-on independent legshield sides, which, in case of damage, could be quickly and cheaply replaced. Air intake for the carburettor was via the centre tube of the frame, right from the front of the scooter where it was cooler and thus better for combustion. The suspension was simple, cheap and effective, making use of rubber blocks. The wheels were split rim, making for simple puncture repair.

The Tina appeared in March 1962 at a retail price of £94. (There wasn't a BSA-badged version as there had been with the Tigress.) The engine was a 100cc, two-stroke unit producing 4.5bhp. The gearbox was similar to that of the Manurhin in that it used a belt drive which rode higher up the sides of a rotating pulley as speed increased. The footbrake was mounted across the centre of the footboard so that it could be used by either foot. The only handlebar

# tu nueva conquista

**Lambretta**

A Triumph T10 tricycle beside a Triumph T10 scooter.

Triumph Tina and Ariel Three at a rally near Yeovil in Somerset.

controls were for the lights, a start/drive switch, throttle, and front brake. Plastic was used for the front mudguard, and the exhaust system was a simple and cheap to make tubular motorcycle-type.

A wide range of accessories was offered, including windscreen carrier, pannier bags, chrome wheel discs, and front-mounted shopping basket.

As was unfortunately true of many British companies then, production began before full development had been completed. Also, the general public, was not quite ready to accept the idea of an automatic gearbox. Many accidents resulted from engines being revved in order to hear its note, the revver not appreciating that doing this whilst the scooter was in drive mode would cause it to shoot off at relatively high speed, invariably damaging the delicate front plastic mudguard. Another drawback of the system was that the scooter could not be pushed-started; in fact, if there was a problem with the engine it was very difficult, if not impossible, to push at all. A design flaw in the automatic clutch meant it could lock solid, with disastrous results. An electrical system was designed to cut the engine if it exceeded a certain speed in start mode, but, as the contacts wore, settings became disturbed and gave more problems with starting.

Quality control problems at the factory concerned kickstarter quadrants and gear wheels which wore out in a very short time, resulting in jamming and slipping. The petrol filler cap had been positioned just behind the seat, and quite often clothing would be soiled by oil and petrol.

## now... you can **all** get about...

easy... easier... EASIEST! Yes, TRIUMPH AUTOMATIC is, wi doubt the easiest to handle o vehicles, power or pedal, two wh or four. It has two controls only twistgrip accelerator and brakes you've been accustomed to a clutch gears you'll be amazed at the driving technique you get with no clutch, no-gears Triumph A matic — the all-purpose family veh

## TRIUMPH
AUTOMATIC T

It wasn't long before initial good sales trailed off to virtually none at all as word of these shortcomings spread. The British motorcycle industry was going through a terrible time with prospective customers deserting to buy the superior Japanese machines that filled the market.

Triumph understood the situation and made a concerted effort to sort things out with the scooter. The automatic gearbox clutch was redesigned with rectangular wedges rather than ball bearings, which overcame the jamming. A complete redesign of the bodywork followed so that, in 1965, the Triumph T10 scooter replaced the Tina.

The T10 was a much better machine, though, sadly, with its own quality control problems. The start/drive switch was now sited under the seat and activated by the pressure of the rider's body, which still gave rise to some problems but was an improvement. The fuel cap was now also under the seat, where it did no harm; the front mudguard was made of steel, and chromium plating smartened the appearance.

The T10 had a difficult time trying to shake off the Tina's reputation, and sales were not as good as Triumph had hoped. As with its predecessor – and so many British scooters – insufficient time had been given over to full development of the machine before it went on sale.

The last T10 left the production line in 1970 after a reasonable sales life (for the period). There were plans to produce a three-wheeled version that incorporated a flat, load-carrying area at the rear. On cornering, its ingenious design would allow the front to lean whilst the rear remained flat. Ten prototypes were made but production did not follow. Years later, this concept was developed by the Japanese and produced in various forms, including the Honda Stream.

Today, machines of similar size to the T10 and Tina are automatic and use plastic in their bodywork. The little Triumphs were a foretaste of the future, though sadly, not for British production.

### Vespa Rally 180

Of all the scooter manufacturers, Piaggio is the one

A Vespa Rally 180 at a transport rally at Hengrove in Bristol.

that deserves the most thanks for resurrecting the scooter after the Second World War. This company instigated a whole new chapter of economic transport for the new generation.

Piaggio's first offering in the early 1950s was rather like the Piatti but without its smooth curves. The first true Vespa was produced in 1946, since when its shape has changed little. It is just still possible to buy a modern Vespa equipped with manual gear change, which closely resembles the basic original design with the engine situated off-centre, directly driving the rear wheel, without the need for chains or shaft drive. This makes for very quick and snappy engine response, making Vespa riding a unique pleasure. Today, though, it is likely that the scooter offered will be of Indian manufacture, no longer carrying that proud Italian name.

As the world has moved on Piaggio began to manufacture Vespas with low pollution four-stroke engines and automatic gearboxes. In theory an offset engine is not a design ideal, but in practice it seems to matter little, and millions of sales worldwide indicate many satisfied customers who continue to buy the original Vespa design. The scooter has been produced under licence in many different countries around the world, and without licence in others, including Russia, whose Vjatka is an almost exact copy of the 1950s Vespa GS!

Today, the Vespa is known under different names depending in which country it is produced. Italy – its birthplace – has produced the most examples over the years, but now countries like India have manufactured so many in recent years under different names, including Bajaj, that production figures have surpassed the Italians'.

The Vespa began life with a 98cc engine, though very soon the most popular capacity was 125cc and later 150cc. As the scooter market expanded, however, there was a need for a special, high performance model, and the 150cc Vespa GS (Grand Sport: probably the most revered initials in classic scooter history) was born in 1955, available in metallic silver and sporting larger, 10 inch wheels.

Piaggio continued to manufacture a Vespa with a little extra something in addition to its regular range, and in 1962 produced a 160cc version of the GS. The internal mechanics of the Vespa continued to evolve and become more efficient, and Piaggio became well known for the advances it made in two-stroke design, including introduction of rotary valve engines. In 1964 the top performance model had a 180cc engine

*A rain-soaked Vespa Rally 180 at a scooter parts fayre in Market Harborough, Leicestershire.*

## go on - tempt yourself...

## ...to a Vespa Rally

Fall for a Vespa and it will become the apple of your eye and the envy of your friends.

Vespa, the spur of the moment transport that sets you free to indulge your whims of fancy—your transport of delight.

World wide, more Vespa's are sold than any other make. Vespa plan to hold this lead in the future by always offering the best engineering, the best design, the best performance in scooters.

Now ! five models to choose from : Vespa 90 for gentle relaxing cruising ; Vespa 90 Racer for the discerning sportsman ; Vespa 125 Super for that extra zest : Vespa 150 Super the go everywhere scooter : and the Vespa Rally 180 for high speed super sports performance.

**Get the zest out of life with a Vespa—there's magic in the world of Vespa.**

and the famous GS initials were dropped in favour of SS – for Super Sport! This engine developed 10.3bhp – about three times that of the first Vespa.

By 1968 the high performance model had become the Rally 180, developing 12bhp, and was available primarily in a tangerine colour (later also in yellow) which set it apart from other scooters. It was capable of 60mph and used the relatively low, 2 per cent cleaner two-stroke oil mixture. It was the first Vespa to lose some of the side panel bulge, looking more modern in the process. In spite of this the spare wheel could still be carried within the left panel, which helped to balance the weight of the offset engine on the other side. There was a good-sized lockable compartment behind the front legshield; the bike's suspension was stiffened and improved, the dualseat was firm, and the headlamp larger than on previous models.

Young people of the day seemed particularly attracted to the model and it became something of a cult symbol of independent youth! The sales brochure for the Vespa Rally 180 described it as "... a new formula in the field of sport scooters."

<A>s a teenager in the 1960s, my first microcar was a Messerschmitt. Having ridden a scooter for some time, I wanted my own more comfortable, covered transport, and a conventional car was way out of my reach. Also, there was no way I could have afforded driving lessons for a car licence, and my existing scooter licence permitted me to drive a microcar, provided reverse gear was blanked off. (This didn't cause a problem as it was easy enough to push it backward if necessary.)

I thought the Messerschmitt's design made it stand out from the crowd and it appeared to be the transport of the future. It was very aerodynamic; its small size and weight meant it didn't need a large engine, so was economic to drive, and it did not need much space in which to park. Being single, just one passenger seat suited me fine, and without a passenger there was plenty of room behind the driving seat for suitcases and other luggage.

The Messerschmitt was fun to drive and had a much livelier performance than its engine size suggested: the heater was much appreciated in winter. Passengers sat behind the driver with their legs each side of the driving seat. The transparent dome gave excellent all-round vision and was very cosy in winter, though liable to cause cabin overheating in better weather. (Cabriolet versions didn't have this problem.) The sliding side windows could be removed completely if required.

The Messerschmitt's main drawback was that when ascending long hills it got slower and slower, though was quite capable of keeping up with normal traffic on the single carriageway roads of the time.

In the 1980s I restored a Heinkel bubblecar and that rewarded me with new motoring experiences.

Isettas and Bond Bugs at Portishead.

# Why get wet?

At last! The CABIN SCOOTER is the answer to all those 'rainy day' problems. You will travel in warmth, comfort and safety both for business and pleasure. Such manoeuvrability enables easy parking, and petrol — you'd hardly notice — at 85 miles per gallon.

**Standard Model** . . . . . . . £276-6-2 plus £66-12-8 P.T.
**De Luxe Model** . . . . . . . £295-18-1 plus £71-6-3 P.T.

*H.P. arrangements available at your dealers.*

# CABIN SCOOTERS LTD.

### SOLE CONCESSIONAIRES IN THE UNITED KINGDOM

## 17 GREAT CUMBERLAND PLACE, LONDON, W.1

A Messerschmitt KR200 near Bossington Beach, West Somerset.

Its single front door and perfect teardrop shape was very appealing. There was plenty of room inside for driver and passenger on the front bench seat, and also room for two children or luggage on the smaller seat behind. In the winter the large bubble could have misting problems and, because the engine was situated within the dome, noise levels were high.

Its four-stroke engine was reliable and easy to start. Filling up with fuel did not require the mixing of oil. It was, however, relatively difficult to work on the engine as lifting the rear cowl only really exposed the rear wheel. To adjust the points great patience was required – and the help of a mirror!

In the summer the fabric roof could be folded back, which was much appreciated. If reverse was unavailable in your particular car, care was needed not to park too close to another vehicle or other solid structure or it would not be possible to get out of the car! The brakes left a lot to be desired for the modern

*SEEING*
*is*
*believing*

If you are ready for a change, ...

and a *TRIAL RUN will convince you that YOU CAN'T BEAT the*

## NEW LINE 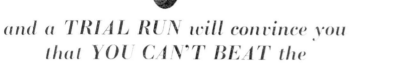 250 G

*some of the outstanding features . . .*
* *New Styling*   * *Lockheed hydraulic braking system*
* *Opening Quarter windows*   * *Larger Wheels*
* *Winding windows*   * *Locking doors*
* *New Villiers engine developing 11·4 B.H.P.*
* *And New all round independent suspension with hydraulic shock-absorbers*

... drive to ...

... your nearest smart Centre. ...

... In no time at all

*Bond*
**Minicar**
"MARK C"

... we'll exchange the bodypanels ..

... for a different colour.

**100 M P G**

WITH THE AMAZING 4-PASSENGER HEINKEL

world, and had a tendency to pull the car to one side when operated. Hard braking in an emergency was reminiscent of a wrestling match, and because of the front door it was a difficult car to push-start.

A heater was fitted, and, besides air flow, it allowed much more noise into the cabin, it was commonplace for owners to literally put a sock in it! (the outlet).

During restoration of the Heinkel some spare parts were just not available, which is where imagination and skill were required to get over the problem. Club membership was invaluable in this respect.

My 1980s Messerschmitt

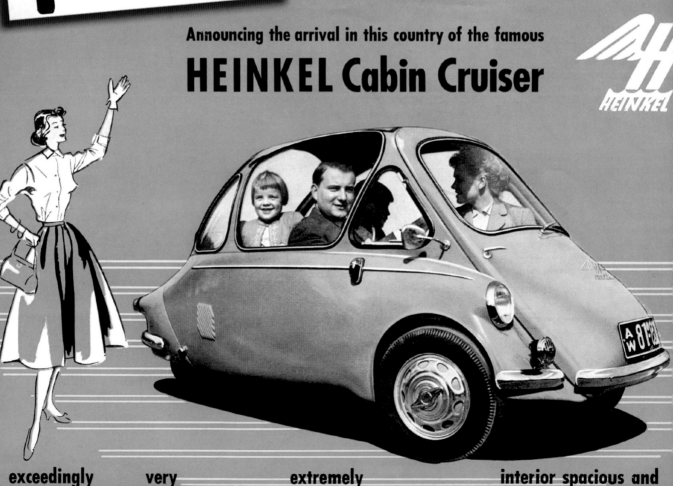

TRAVEL IN STYLE FOR A PENNY A MILE

Announcing the arrival in this country of the famous

# HEINKEL Cabin Cruiser

exceedingly **FAST**      very **MOBILE**      extremely **ECONOMICAL**      interior spacious and **COMFORTABLE**

restoration did not throw up any significant spare part supply difficulties, and the owner's club offered excellent backup and a magazine. Some spares were expensive, however, and vital in the restoration. My first driving impression after a break of thirty years was how little suspension buffering there was from contact with rough roads. The direct and sensitive handle bar steering was a skill which had to be re-learnt ... The brakes were hardly up to the standard now required for modern traffic, and, because of its low height, driving on modern motorways was a little daunting. Long hills were still a drag – literally (this applies to all of the sixties microcars with little engines). It was still fun to drive, though.

The Bond Minicar restoration in

GET OUT AND ABOUT WITH A **Trojan** '200'

TROJAN LIMITED · TROJAN WORKS · PURLEY WAY · CROYDON · SURREY

*Now, and then. A Smart Passion and ... an Isetta; 40 years separate these designs.*

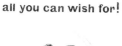

the 1990s brought its own unique experiences. Back in the 1960s, Bonds were about on the roads and had been for a decade; like motorcycles with sidecars, they were an established and accepted alternative form of transport. At the time they did not appeal to me, mostly because of insufficient exhaust silencing. They appeared crude, and did not possess the more modern style and design of the new bubblecars.

The later, mid-1960s mark G minicars did, however, offer the much quieter, more powerful and smoother Villiers 2T twin engine, and the driving cabin was more user-friendly. Capable of carrying four people and their luggage, it also had the big bonus of a very accessible engine. It was possible to step in under the bonnet and work on the engine with no complications associated with fan cooling; every part was there in the open. Actually, the engine was mounted on top of the front wheel, so it turned with the steering, allowing the car to be reversed within the space of its own length. A kickstarter was also available in case of a flat battery.

Headlamps were large and efficient enough for night-time use, but the minicar's design meant it did not have a heater, which was a problem in the winter. I remember watching ice form on the inside of the windscreen, gradually obscuring my vision on one particular winter journey. On the road the steering felt more like that of a boat than a car, although a long wheelbase did make it feel quite stable, and, as power was not used for a fan, performance was quite good, as were the hydraulically-controlled brakes. Again, the roof could be opened right up in the summertime, which was very nice. Spares were generally freely available, especially for the Villiers engines which, of course, were used for many years on a great variety of British motorcycles.

In the late 1990s the Smart was announced with a new, specially-developed, three-cylinder, 600cc engine from Mercedes, a modern resurrection of the microcar, but with no compromises in safety, performance or facilities. The specification is truly amazing for a little car. It has ABS, traction control, air conditioning and a turbocharger. It combines maximum economy with style, convenience (it can be parked where most other cars can't), and performance.

It was a gamble which has paid off well. Other modern microcars have followed but do not have the same winning Smart formula. Many enthusiasts imported their cars years ago from the continent in left-hand drive before they were officially available in the UK. I remember mine causing quite a stir when first seen on local roads. A child was heard asking his father what it was, and he replied that it must be a bubblecar from the 1960s ...

A truly useful and stylish update of the microcar, the Smart's only drawback is a rather bouncy ride over rough surfaces, due to a short wheelbase.

Today, its manufacturer also successfully commissions several specially-tuned Brabus performance versions of the Smart, and made another small roadster design, the Smart Roadster, like the microcars of the 1960s. Sadly, this model was not destined for a long life and produduction has now ended. Sales were not as extensive as had been hoped, most probably because the retail price was too high, putting it out of reach of the young people who would have loved to own one.

*A Bond Minicar estate MK G at the Haynes Transport Museum in Sparkford, Somerset.*

# Scooter ownership

What sort of people were the first scooter owners back in the 1950s, and what sort of lives did they lead? An idea of the answers to these questions can be had from the pictures painted by the adverts of the time. Being a Piatti owner, and a lad of seventeen, I was particularly intrigued by the advert depicting a carefree, adventurous young lady setting off to see the world on her scooter. There was also an advert showing a scantily-clad Miss scooting past an old-fashioned chap on a motorbike in full wet weather gear. What a fresh and modern image the scooter had compared to the motorcycle!

Scooter magazines had a strong influence on the enthusiast, who would eagerly read them from cover-to-cover. Adverts were very much part of the scene and avidly scanned for news about new machines and accessories to fit on them. If you read, for example, about a new, lockable storage box you could fit onto a carrier, off you went to see one at your nearest dealer, as advertised in the magazine. The Raydyot Scootboot was a very useful addition to have. Today, it would be called a top box, which is waterproof, lightweight, and available in all shapes and sizes; then, it was a new idea and there was only the one make. Initially available in only one colour scheme – light blue with a silver lid – the box was made of steel, so was therefore rather heavy: early examples were also liable to leak at the base. Sitting, as it did, at the rear of the scooter, it had an adverse affect on handling, even when empty. But it did – for the first time – offer a lockable compartment for shopping and a safe place to store a crash helmet; a great idea that made the scooter even more useful and user-friendly.

An NSU Prima advert of 1957 showed how a scooter would be ideal transport for a smart family man, perhaps for going to work or for travelling on business, complete with trilby hat! In the early days crash helmets were thought to be something that most people didn't really need to bother about, though perhaps one was needed on a motorbike. It wasn't necessary on a scooter as they were much more civilised! There was a very lighthearted approach to safety in general; it was never suggested that a rider might come off his scooter, or that he might need protective headwear and clothing if he did. It was much more fun to feel the wind in your hair, anyway, and any talk of accidents was thought to be 'square' and pessimistic. It was okay to casually suggest that care be taken when riding in the wet, but no more than that. Cars were certainly not routinely fitted with seat belts and, if riders of fast motorcycles wore a hat at all, very often it would be a cloth cap!

"Travel far and wide" exclaims a Lambretta advert, showing a girl with a fully loaded scooter,

continued page 117

110

**What sort of people rode**

**scooters in the 50's and 60's?**

**Spree**

Going Places .. Finding Fun .. Living

**A Miss with a Purpose ..**

SHE KNOWS HER WAY AROUND—
AND WHAT BETTER WAY THAN ON A

**SCOOTER**

## go man go!!...

Get with it and plunge for a fabulous 'Capella'. From a low powered 148cc to the 200cc de-luxe model the D.K.R. 'Capella' is renowned for reliability and performance. Sleek...smooth...immaculate... economical, it is a machine which every rider will be proud to possess.

| | | |
|---|---|---|
| 148cc Capella Mark 1 | .... | £144 9 6 |
| 173cc Capella Standard | .... | £152 13 6 |
| 173cc Capella De-Luxe | .... | £166 10 0 |
| (electric start) | | |
| 200cc Capella Kick Start | .... | £164 11 0 |
| 200cc Capella De-Luxe | .... | £173 13 10 |
| (electric start) | | |

All prices include Purchase Tax

.. by  "**Capella**"

POWERED BY **Villiers** ENGINES

*Post this coupon for illustrated folder*
**D.K.R. SCOOTERS LTD.**
WODEN ROAD, WOLVERHAMPTON

Name ........................................
Address ....................................
........................................ B.19

**The finest,** **smoothest,**
**most modern**
**form of**
**economical**
**travel**

**prima**
MOTOR SCOOTER

For real luxury two-wheel travel-comfort, road-holding and stability—the sleek, streamlined 'PRIMA' is in a class by itself, for a 150 c.c. engine and three-speed gearbox give lively acceleration and exceptional hill climbing; power transmission is by shaft drive just like a car, while powerful smooth-acting brakes provide remarkable stopping power. The 'PRIMA' is supplied complete with electric self-starter, pillion seat, carrier, spare wheel, 12 volt lighting and many extras for £198. 6s. 9d. (incl. P. Tax £38. 7s. 9d.)

*★ NOTHING BETTER ON TWO WHEELS*

*See your local dealer today or write to us for catalogue S11.*

**NSU (GREAT BRITAIN) LTD.** 7 Chesterfield Gardens, London, W.1

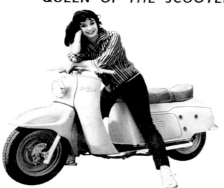

SINGLE BOY

TRIUMPH MOTORROLLER

INTERESTED IN THE GIRLS!

UNSURPASSABLE

The man that **gets ahead** gets there on a **Vespa** Gran Sport

THE SLEEKEST, MOST POWERFUL MACHINE OF ITS CLASS

**The Gran Sport:**
150 c.c. powerful, dependable high-efficiency engine . . . surpassing all other machines of its class with 60 m.p.h. peak performance.

- Direct drive to rear wheel.
- Side mounted engine for cheaper, easier maintenance and leg protection.
- Low gravity centre for road holding stability—perfect balance.
- The leading make with a 12 months' guarantee.
- Nation and world wide Vespa Dealer network for spares and service.
- Superb, full range of practical accessories.

cash **£188·8·3** (inc. P.T.)

or **£37·13·6** deposit and 25/6 per week over 3 years.

**Douglas**
(Sales and Service) Ltd.

Division of Westinghouse Brake and Signal Co. Ltd., who employ some 11,000 British people.

Get ahead - see your Vespa dealer right away

**POST TODAY** Douglas (Sales and Service) Ltd., Kingswood, Bristol.
Please send me more information on Vespa. S.W.3.

Mr./Mrs./Miss...........................

Address..........................

BLOCK CAPITALS

Vespa

Mit der Zeit gehen!

*Goggo* ... fahren

The *Scintillating* **BSA SUNBEAM**

15 COE

LES
*scooters* Peugeot *1956*

CIÉTÉ "CYCLES PEUGEOT" · BEAULIEU-VALENTIGNEY (DOUBS)

THE NEW
125cc. *Piatti*

## Sun Wasp
**173 cc.**

*Quality with Design*

ELECTRIC AND KICK ST...

SCOOTER DE...

VOK 272

IT'S HERE...THE TRIUMPH **tina**

*the worlds first fully automatic scooter at less than £100!*

100 %
BRITISH
AND STILL
THE BEST

*Feel Proud...*
Buy
PHOENIX

H. B. ENGINEER...
(DEPT. P.P.)
34 COMMERCE...
LONDON N...
BOWES PARK...

standard : £147 . 4 . 0 inc. p.t.

de luxe : £157 . 10 . 0 inc. p.t.

Scooter
Peugeot

GM4

LA PETITE AUTO A 2 ROUES ET A 2 PLACES

presumably on a European tour. It was the done thing, then, because scooters offered a really cheap way of crossing the Channel; you could even put it on a plane and fly across. The cost of going to France was not much more putting your scooter on a train within the UK. (Modern regulations do not allow this now.)

The ladies were a particular target for the advertisers. Previously, there was hardly any point in advertising to the fairer sex as most would not have been interested in a conventional motorcycle with its associated oil, dirt and unglamorous clothing. The scooter made a style statement and offered a feminine way of being seen and appreciated by the opposite sex. And, of course, it provided weather protected transport for going to the shops or on an evening out. Larger cinemas had their own covered parking areas for scooters, and sometimes there was an attendant to look after them whilst you enjoyed the films.

A BSA Dandy advert portrayed how easy it was to simply sit on a scooter, ride off and travel for hundreds of miles; I think this was a little optimistic as the Dandy was not the ideal scooter to cover long distances on, though certainly scooters of 125cc and above were often used in that way. Nevertheless, the advertising did what it intended by getting riders to think of their scooters as being capable of this: if you needed to journey far, just get on your bike and off you go – as simple as that – a freedom revolution.

The Guizzo advert of 1958 showed two girls on the one scooter. Travelling two-up did slow the scooter on hills, but at least it gave the freedom to take off with a friend. The manufacturer of even more powerful scooters such as the Maicoletta hoped to attract women riders by describing the machine as the 'Queen of Scooters', a title also used later by Zundapp Bella.

Boy meets girl on a Raleigh Roma! Boys were told that girls liked scooters and girls liked boys who ride scooters, all very true but boys also liked girls who had their own scooters. If one thing led to another and you became an item, then a Bond minicar was the answer. Think of the fun that could be had on the bench seat (Messerschmitt owners perhaps missed out here due to having single seats, one behind the other). And for your golfing interests an Open Bond or a Messerschmitt was the perfect choice,

as there was certainly room for a golf bag or two and a change of clothing.

Exploiting every opportunity, one advert showed how a Messerschmitt could easily accommodate and transport you and your dog.

In terms of attractively portraying a stylish image and lifestyle that a scooter could bestow – at the tennis court, on the beach, camping, or shopping, suggesting where and how owners might use their scooters to get the most from them – it is hard to beat the range of wonderful colour shots used by Lambretta in its sales brochures and magazine adverts of 1959. The use of colour in advertising was relatively new then and really made an impact. Magazine readers identified with the kind of people featured in the adverts and wanted that lifestyle for themselves.

Happy people, happy scootering!

St. Gotthard

Simplon

Riva

Roma

ce

London

München

*Diana* THE ACME OF PER

LE SCOOTER BIPLACE *Peugeot* MODÈLE S. 55

whichever way you look at it...

**Moby** scooter

Is the *better* scooter!

Oslo

Paris

## ISO GETS THERE FIRST!

**THE SCOOTER WITH THE ATOMIC PERFORMANCE**

## ISO
### MILANO DE-LUXE

Whether for work or pleasure the ISO c.c. ISO Scooter meets your every requirement for this modern age. Beautifully designed, this precision-made machine offers a magnificent performance with the utmost economy and reliability. Combining superb suspension, light positive steering, fantastic roadholding and powerful brakes, the ISO will delight the enthusiast and novice alike.

AT A DOWN-TO-EARTH PRICE £166-19-6 (INCLUDING)

WRITE NOW FOR **FREE** ILLUSTRATED CATALOGUE AND ADDRESS OF YOUR NEAREST AGENT

**STUART & PAYNE LTD., 6 7 Bankside, London, S.E.1**

## JOIN THE 'JET-SET' ON A Lambretta

**THE JET SET**

## Lambretta
### luna
### vega
### cometa

# A-Z of popular scooters and microcars

The specification details in this chapter should not be taken too literally, as manufacturers exaggerated a lot of the claims. It seemed to be common practice to increase the quoted top speed figures by ten per cent, for example, and nobody was very inclined to challenge these claims. Very often manufacturers did not publish a full specification for their vehicles, in any case, and brochures did not normally give such details as it was considered that prospective owners weren't that interested. Nor was this information even given in the manuals that came with the machines. Details of the bhp power rating of the various engines was sometimes thought to be a trade secret, which competitors shouldn't know. Neither did manufacturers want their customers to be too concerned with this aspect.

If a machine was somewhat overweight, manufacturers did not want to publicise that fact either. In order to qualify for a lower level of road tax, three-wheelers had specific upper weight restrictions, and most were constructed to the very upper limit of these. Sometimes, even a magazine road test report – which, today, would be a searching investigation – did not mention specific figures (which explains why there are many 'unknowns' in the following microcar weight entries).

Wherever possible, I have given independent magazine test figures for the data, as these should be closer to the truth.

I remember being surprised that my first scooter only ever managed a maximum of 40mph as the brochure did mention speeds of up to 45mph. If that machine was indeed capable of achieving such a speed, it would only have been with no windscreen or luggage, a much smaller and lighter person than me aboard – and a following tailwind! Even today some incredible figures are bandied about by owners regarding the top speed and fuel consumption of their restorations!

In quite a few cases I have not been able to find official figures for these two specifications, which gives some idea of how unimportant such details were considered to be: buying a scooter or microcar meant ownership of a unique and individual vehicle, and specifications like this were of little consequence to the buyer.

As scooters and microcars became more popular, road tests began to feature in motorcycle magazines as well as in scooter publications. As weekly publications, motorcycle magazines were often first on the bookstalls with the latest news, and were favoured by manufacturers as a result. They also employed some superb artists who would produce excellent, accurate sectioned drawings of a new machine, a feature seldom seen today.

Road tests of microcars featured mostly in car magazines, so were not usually read by prospective microcar owners, whose primary interest was economy of purchase price, road tax and fuel consumption. A conventional car was very much more expensive in all of these areas. Prospective microcar purchasers were usually either first-time buyers or ex-scooter, motorcycle and sidecar riders looking for more comfort and convenience at minimum cost.

The choice of machine tested was sometimes a curious one. Very often a magazine would test an unusual vehicle, only for another publication to road test the very same machine a short while later. It would seem that a manufacturer or importer offered the machine to several periodicals to road test, all of whom accepted instead of finding their own to feature. Sometimes the tests were so similar it seemed as if the same person had done them and then written slightly different reports for the two publications ...

The fact that unusual machines often featured in road tests could give the wrong impression today of what was popular and seen on the roads then. I remember reading about, amongst others, the Sim Ariete, Goggo, Hausman Rodeo, Osa, and Rumi Socoittolo, but never encountered any of these at clubs, on rallies, or on the road. Other models – such as the Mercury Pippin and the Britax Scooterette – would occasionally be seen but I suspect that actual sales were very low. Even the Phoenix, which had a wide range of engine capacities and was in production for a long period, made very little impression on the streets, at least away from the London area where it was made. Very often with some machines their press coverage was out of proportion to their appearance on the roads.

What comes across from looking at the photos of all the different makes and models of the late 1950s and early 1960s is the wonderful range and diversity of design. Just ten years later enthusiasts were limited to a choice of only two makes of scooter, Lambretta and Vespa, leading to fierce competition between owners. In the good old days of the late '50s there was plenty of choice and variety for everyone, and scooterists felt united in a common bond, although there still existed a feeling of superiority amongst owners of the big two – and perhaps for good reason ...

Magazines kept us informed about the interesting machines in other countries that were not available in the UK. The names of some were interesting, too: how about the Bastert, the Autoflug, the Bugre, and the Bombadier!

Some of the machines that were available in the UK also had unusual names; the Rumi Little Ant, for example. What incredible machines they were, too. It was possible to place a coin on edge on the crankcase and rev the engine without disturbing the coin; I saw this done and can verify the truth of the claim. True, it was an old three-penny bit, which had a broad, flat edge but it was still an impressive demonstration.

Some scooters were advertised which never seemed to take off in the UK, like the Bitri from Holland. It looked good, and had the same engine as that fitted in the Messerschmitt bubblecar, so should have been an excellent machine. The Progress from Germany was a similar example; a few were produced in the UK using locally-made fibreglass bodywork, yet they achieved very few sales. I think the manufacturer of this machine was of the opinion that advertising was  not necessary, which is why so few were sold.

Then there was the Harley-Davidson Topper – a very rare American import – an automatic with adequate power, yet hardly any UK sales. Interesting scooters were being made in Japan, such as the Fuji Rabbit and the Mitsubishi Silver Pigeon, but no attempt was made to sell them in the UK. Perhaps it was just as well for the sake of our own industry ...

Sometimes, a new model would be announced in the press and road tested. If it was developed from an earlier model, it would be claimed that the problems and limitations of the original, as with the Piatti, had been overcome, yet the new model never reached the showrooms and the manufacturer simply faded away, leaving the enthusiast rather let down and somewhat bewildered!

Have a look through the following pages – arranged in alphabetical order – and wonder at the range that was available.

*Thanks to Martin Round for photos of the Capri 150, Sim Ariete and Swallow Gadabout, Andy Gillard for the Catria and Harper, and John Churchill for the Bond P4. I am grateful to Robin Spalding for allowing me access to his wonderful collection of restored classic scooters, which continues to grow.*

# Scooters

## ABC Skootamota (UK) 1920

ABC 125cc 4-stroke engine
1-speed gearbox and 16 inch wheels
Maximum speed: 15mph/24kph
Weight: unknown
ABC was a very patriotic company; its initials stood for 'All British Cycle'. Produced from 1919 to 1923, the Skootmota achieved good sales figures. Many were exported to other countries; France, for example, took 1000 examples. There was no clutch – you ran with it to start the engine – and then jumped on when it was going! It was capable of only modest performance but set the trend for the future.

## Adler Junior (West Germany) 1956

Adler 98cc 2-stroke 4bhp engine
3-speed gearbox and 3.00 x 14 wheels
Maximum speed: 43mph/70kph
Weight: 220lb/95kg
Introduced in 1955, the Junior was heavy for a small-engined scooter, but did have a 12v electric starter as standard. Adler had previously produced bicycles and two-stroke motorcycles with engine sizes ranging from 98cc to 250cc. It also produced a range of office equipment, including typewriters. The company was taken over by Grundig in 1958 and from then on all vehicle production ceased.

## Agrati Capri (Italy) 1960

Garelli 80cc 2-stroke 3.8bhp engine
3-speed gearbox and 3.00 x 12 wheels
Maximum speed: 40mph/64kph
Weight: 165lb/75kg
This model became very popular in the UK, being one of the first small engine capacity scooters to appear. It retailed at less than that of a Vespa or Lambretta as it was simpler in design. The first models had spoked wheels. Its 12 inch wheels did provide better stability than the 8 inch version that many other makes still used. It was later available in 70cc, 98cc, 125cc, and 150cc versions.

### Agrati Capri Super 150 (Italy) 1965

Garelli 153cc 2-stroke 7.5bhp engine
4-speed gearbox and 3.00 x 12 wheels
Maximum speed: 50mph/80kph
Weight: 210lb/95kg

Unlike earlier small capacity Capris, this model has a fully enclosed, double drive chain running in an oil bath. The length adjuster is situated externally, which is very useful compared to the similar Lambretta drive system. Overall weight is quite light for a 150cc so acceleration is reasonable compared to the opposition. The entire rear bodywork lifts clear for maintenance. This was the ultimate Capri model which is very rare today.

### Ambassador (UK) 1961

Villiers 173cc 2-stroke 7.5bhp engine
4-speed gearbox and 3.50 x 10 wheels
Maximum speed: 53mph/85kph
Weight: 272lb/123kg

Ambassador used to successfully import and distribute the German Zundapp Bella scooter but mistakenly thought it could make a better scooter than the Bella and sell more using a British Villiers engine. The scooter is probably the only surviving example, and somewhere in its history the side panels became lost.

### Avro Monocar (UK) 1926

Villiers 250cc 2-stroke engine
3-speed gearbox and large wheels
Maximum speed: unknown
Weight: unknown

A prototype that did not reach production. It was years ahead of its time in being a large-wheeled scooter with an aluminium body on a pressed steel frame, fitted with a large engine and shaft drive. It was designed by an aircraft engineer who wanted something more comfortable and user-friendly than a conventional motorcycle to get to work on. This example survives today in the UK's Science Museum.

## Bernadet (France) 1953
Bernadet 250cc 2-stroke engine
4-speed gearbox and 3.50 x 12 wheels
Maximum speed: unknown
Weight: 219lb/95kg
The Bernadet was not imported to the UK but this one has been brought into the country in recent years by a collector who liked its unique style. The Y52 model is called the Texas, and is adorned with a saddle complete with cowboy tassels and studs. There were also rhinestone saddle bags, and the handlebars had tassels hanging from the ends. Many other Bernadet models existed, of various engine sizes, all with individual style.

## Binz (West Germany) 1957
Sachs 49cc 2-stroke 1.6bhp engine
2-speed gearbox and 2.25 x 20 wheels
Maximum speed: 28mph/45kph
Weight: 88lb/49kg
The Binz company made bodies for commercial vehicles, and in 1954 produced a scooter. Initial choice was between an Ilo pull-start or a Sachs kickstart engine. The kickstart version was available in the UK only between late 1956 and 1957. Note the novel position for the headlamp. A speedometer was an extra.

## Bitri (The Netherlands) 1957
Ilo 150cc 2-stroke 6.7bhp engine
4-speed gearbox and 4.00 x 8 wheels
Maximum speed: unknown
Weight: 225lb/103kg
The Bitri appeared in 1954 with a 118cc, 4.5bhp Ilo engine and 2-speed gearbox. In 1957 it was also possible to specify the Sachs 197cc, 10.2bhp engine. Produced in a small factory, the Bitri did not achieve large sales, though was briefly available in the UK, where it deserved to sell rather better than it did by virtue of the Sachs engine which performed so well in the Prior scooter and Messerschmitt bubblecar. Production ceased in the early 1960s.

## Bond Minibyke (UK) 1951

JAP 125cc 2-stroke engine
3-speed gearbox and 4.00 x 16 wheels
Maximum speed: unknown
Weight: 112lb/51kg

The oval section frame of the Minibyke was made
of aluminium. Initially, without suspension front or
rear, rider comfort was dependent on the sprung seat.
The wheels did have split rims for relatively easy
tyre replacement. Early models used a 99cc, Villiers
engine with a 2-speed gearbox. The last examples
were made in 1953. Note the early use of the name
Mini in Bond products, later famous for the Bond
Minicars.

## Bond P2 (UK) 1959

Villiers 197cc 2-stroke 8.4bhp engine
4-speed gearbox and 4.00 x 10 wheels
Maximum speed: 58mph/93kph
Weight: 274lb/124kg

The P1 used a 150cc Villiers engine with a 3-speed
gearbox. This and the P2 had fibreglass bodywork
which included a useful glovebox behind the
legshields. Styling was very reminiscent of a 1950s
American motor, and probably appreciated more
today than it was then. The front end of the 150cc P3
and 197cc P4 was restyled in 1960 to be more beak-
like, losing a degree of character in the process.

## Bond P4 (UK) 1960

Villiers 197cc 2-stroke 8.4bhp engine
4-speed gearbox and 4.00 x 10 wheels
Maximum speed: 58mph/93kph
Weight: 264lb/120kg

This later model featured a redesigned, lighter front
which didn't turn with the wheel. Engine and gearbox
were sited 2.5 inches lower in the frame to improve
roadholding. A 150cc version was also available
called the P3. Fibreglass was still used for bodywork,
which hinged at the rear for good engine access. The
last one left the factory in 1962.

## Brockhouse Corgi (UK) 1948

Excelsior 98cc 2-stroke engine
1-speed gearbox and 2.50 x 8 wheels
Maximum speed: 30mph/48kph
Weight: 95lb/43kg

This was a commercial development of the wartime Welbike used by paratroopers. That machine used a Villiers engine, and was produced by Excelsior. The Corgi used an Excelsior engine and was put together by the Southport-based Brockhouse company under licence. It was the inspiration for the Piatti scooter that appeared some ten years later.

## BSA Dandy (UK) 1957

BSA 70cc 2-stroke 3bhp engine
2-speed gearbox and 20 x 2.5 wheels
Maximum speed: 25mph/40kph
Weight: 100lb/45kg

The Dandy was really halfway between a scooter and a moped, and machines like this were briefly known as Scooterettes. Aavailable colours were red and blue. A bad design feature meant that, in order to adjust the contact breakers, major engine disassembly was necessary. Adjusting the carburettor was also difficult and, unfortunately, these two components did need frequent attention.

## BSA Sunbeam B2s (UK) 1960

BSA 249cc 4-stroke 10bhp engine
4-speed gearbox and 3.50 x 10 wheels
Maximum speed: 63mph/101kph
Weight: 244lb/111kg

This was probably the most successful British scooter design in terms of sales. It was reasonably priced and did offer more engine capacity, plus the freedom from having to mix oil with the petrol. Sadly, it was not fully developed when it went on sale and suffered badly from engine overheating and oil leaks. Side panels were difficult to remove, especially if accessories had been added. The silencer was originally fitted within the bodyshell, often making the side panels too hot to touch. A 175cc, two stroke version later became available based on the Bantam engine.

### Cushman Super Silver Eagle (USA) 1963

Cushman 22cu in 4-stroke 9bhp engine
2-speed gearbox and small wheels
Maximum speed: unknown
Weight: unknown

Cushman was the USA's big name in little wheels, and the Eagle was the last of many scooter designs, sadly, none of which were available in the UK. The first Eagles were produced in 1949 and were really motorcycles with little wheels, but found a good market in the States. Cushman also produced conventional scooters with a flat footboard, and later sold rebadged Vespas.

### Cyclemaster Piatti (UK) 1957

Piatti 125cc 2-stroke 4.7bhp engine
3-speed gearbox and 3.50 x 7 wheels
Maximum speed: 40mph/64kph
Weight: 180lb/82kg

Vincent Piatti was Italian and a true European, working in many different countries. He designed several engines that could be attached to conventional bicycles, which were produced in the UK.  His scooter design was first produced in Belgium. When sales dipped there, production ceased and then restarted in the UK with a few design changes although it needed more. The Mark 2, which should have been a real success, was announced just a month or two before the company ceased production.

### Dayton Albatross (UK) 1956

Villiers 224cc 2-stroke 9.4bhp engine
4-speed gearbox and 4.00 x 12 wheels
Maximum speed: 63mph/101kph
Weight: 310lb/140kg

Dayton was a pedal cycle manufacturer which, before the 1939/44 war, did manufacture motorcycles. It was one of the first British manufacturers to support the scooter idea, in 1955.  The first Albatross had flat legshields and rather crude-looking, open front suspension. It worked and ran well, however, and the design allowed the use of conventional motorcycle engines without the need for fan cooling.

## Dayton Albatross (UK) 1959

Villiers 247cc 2-stroke 15bhp engine
4-speed gearbox and 4.00 x 12 wheels
Maximum speed: 71mph/114kph
Weight: 315lb/143kg

This later Dayton was more appealing to scooterists as the front suspension was covered by stylish panelling. There was a toolbox in the left rear wheel cover, and the 6 volt battery was located in the right one. The handlebar was plain motorcycle-style, and a small glovebox was fitted behind the legshields, the top of which contained – unusually – an ammeter in addition to the speedometer and lighting switch.

## Dayton Albatross (UK) 1960

Villiers 247cc 2-stroke 15bhp engine
4-speed gearbox and 4.00 x 12 wheels
Maximum speed: 71mph/114kph
Weight: 319lb/145kg

This model is considered by many to be the ultimate Dayton. With its twin glovebox and faired-in handlebars, it was set to be a real winner. Unfortunately, Dayton became involved in a takeover which eventually led to it having to pay the debts of another company. This proved its downfall and Dayton closed in 1960. A landmark British scooter!

## Dayton Flamenco (UK) 1959

Villiers 174cc 2-stroke 7.6bhp engine
4-speed gearbox and 3.50 x 10 wheels
Maximum speed: 50mph/80kph
Weight: 305lb/138kg

This was Dayton's smaller scooter, more direct competition to the best-selling Lambrettas and Vespas, but hopefully more appealing to the patriotic home buyer. Some bodywork was shared with the Sun Wasp and the Panther Princess, which were similar in size and used similar engines. The Flamenco died with Dayton in 1960.

## DKR Capella (UK) 1961

Villiers 147cc 2-stroke 6bhp engine
4-speed gearbox and 3.50 x 10 wheels
Maximum speed: 54mph/87kph
Weight: 240lbs/108kg

DKR's earlier scooter designs were not universally appreciated, due largely to a heavy frontal appearance. In 1960, DKR employed a design specialist to come up with something more appealing and modern – the Capella – a giant leap forward in style, and a breath of fresh air which made even the bestselling Lambrettas of the day seem old-fashioned. There's more to a scooter than just style, however, and the Capella had only moderately successful sales. Villiers engine variants were 175cc, 200cc, kick- or electric start.

## DKR Defiant (UK) 1959

Villiers 197cc 2-stroke 8.4bhp engine
4-speed gearbox and 3.50 x 10 wheels
Maximum speed: 59mph/95kph
Weight: 308lb/140kg

A common bodyshell was used for the 1957 kickstart 150cc Dove, the electric start 150cc Pegasus, the electric start Defiant, and 250cc Manx. On the latter model, wider side panels were used to accommodate the larger twin, fan-cooled engine. The fuel tank was situated within the front nose above the front wheel, helping with weight distribution and balance. There was only an electric dynastarter powered by small batteries which was often a problem on short journeys. The last examples were made in 1960.

## DKW Hobby (West Germany) 1956

DKW 75cc 2-stroke 3bhp engine
Auto gearbox and 2.75 x 16 wheels
Maximum speed: 34mph/55kph
Weight: 164lb/75kg

This was Europe's first automatic scooter, which first appeared in 1954. It used a belt system, driving variable diameter cones, the basis of which is still used today. There was a clutch and starting was via a pull handle rather than kickstart. The fuel tap was situated with the choke behind a door at the front of the body. This design was later developed into a full clutchless automatic by the French company, Manurhin.

## DMW Bambi (UK) 1957

Villiers 98cc 2-stroke 2.8bhp engine
2-speed gearbox and 2.50 x 15wheels
Maximum speed: 36mph/58kph
Weight: 165lb/75kg
DMW stood for Dawson's Motors Wolverhampton, a producer of lightweight motorcycles. In 1957 DMW produced its first scooter which had unusually large disc wheels and individual styling, being rather tall and thin. It was rather underpowered so, perhaps was not appealing to many because of that. The 197cc Dumbo variant was a more powerful machine that didn't reach production.

## DMW 1 (UK) 1959

Villiers 175cc 2-stroke 7bhp engine
4-speed gearbox and 3.50 x 10 wheels
Maximum speed: 53mph/85kph
Weight: 242lb/110kg
Sadly, this interesting design was never put into production. It was a think-tank design which could well have appeared with the badging of any of several British manufacturers. Some of the body panels came from other machines and some were new. Negotiations were even under way for production in India. That opportunity was lost to Lambretta which was able to offer greater financial assistance.

## DMW Deemster (UK) 1962

Villiers 247cc 2-stroke 15bhp engine
4-speed gearbox and 4.00 x 12 wheels
Maximum speed: 70mph/113kph
Weight: 350lb/159kg
An upmarket design, which first appeared in 1961, that even offered the option of a roof and built-in windscreen, the idea being to combine the best features of a scooter and a conventional motorcycle. Unfortunately, it cost much more than either machine, so sales were not good. In 1966 the Velocette Viceroy 247cc, flat twin scooter engine could be specified. This special police version had a radio and a blue lamp.

## Ducati Brio 50 (Italy) 1964

Ducati 48cc 2-stroke 4.2bhp engine
3-speed gearbox and 2.75 x 9 wheels
Maximum speed: 25mph/40kph
Weight: 140lb/64kg

Today, few enthusiasts realise that Ducati once made scooters, and little ones at that! Of simple design, they used a small, fan-cooled motorcycle engine with an open chain drive and offered direct competition to the big-selling, small-engined scooters produced by Vespa in Italy. They could be sold at a lower price than the Vespas because of their simpler design.

## Ducati Brio 100 (Italy) 1967

Ducati 94cc 2-stroke 6bhp engine
3-speed gearbox and 3.50 x 8 wheels
Maximum speed: 46mph/76kph
Weight: 187lb/85kg

A more powerful version of the Brio 50; not only was the engine larger, so, too, was the body, although it looked very similar. In 1968 very slightly changed (badging only) versions of both Brios were produced; both models were discontinued in 1969.

## Ducati Cruiser (Italy) 1953

Ducati 175cc 2-stroke engine
Auto gearbox and 3.50 x 10 wheels
Maximum speed: 50mph/80kph
Weight: unknown

The Cruiser was a brilliant design, years ahead of its time. It had an overhead valve, four-stroke engine, and an automatic gearbox similar in design to those used in cars. Its engine was so powerful it had to be detuned for production to meet current regulations. It had an electric starter – unheard of at that time on a two-wheeler. The side panels hinged outward from the front. Unsurprisingly, perhaps, it had a high retail price which limited sales. It was discontinued in 1954.

## Dunkley S65 (UK) 1959

Dunkley 65cc 4-stroke 2.6bhp engine
2-speed gearbox and 2.50 x 15 wheels
Maximum speed: 35mph/56kph
Weight: 165lb/75kg

The Italian company which produced the Casalini
scooter had a surplus of bodies at the end of its
production. Dunkley acquired these, fitted its 65cc
engine, and named the result the Dunkley S65. The
body was unusually designed to hinge open from
the top of the legshields for easy engine access.
Production ceased in 1959, the same year it had
begun. Production did not amount to very many units.

## Durkopp Diana (West Germany) 1956

Durkopp 194cc 2-stroke 9.5bhp engine
4-speed gearbox and 3.50 x 10 wheels
Maximum speed: 50mph/80kph
Weight: 317lb/144kg

The Diana first appeared in 1954 and expanded on
the scooter idea with several luxuries and useful
facilities, such as an electric starter and a kickstarter
with neutral selector built in; the ideal starting
configuration which few others matched. The
headlamp turned with the steering and build quality
was firstclass. The rear brake was controlled by the
right heel which was rather awkward in practice so
later changed to traditional toe operation.

## Durkopp Diana Sport (West Germany) 1960

Durkopp 194cc 2-stroke 10.8bhp engine
4-speed gearbox and 3.50 x 10 wheels
Maximum speed: 59mph/95kph
Weight: 317lb/144kg

This was the ultimate, more powerful Diana which
appeared in 1959. Hot air from the cylinder head was
expelled straight through the left-hand side panel,
which helped with cooling and made for a very
distinctive appearance. It was originally available
in a very bright red colour only, which again made
it stand out from the crowd. Sadly, it later lost these
distinctive features. The last examples were made in
1960.

## Durkopp Diana TS (West Germany) 1960

Durkopp 194cc 2-stroke 9.5bhp engine
4-speed gearbox and 3.50 x 10 wheels
Maximum speed: 58mph/95kph
Weight: 336lb/152kg
With this model Durkopp decided to move the headlamp down to the legshield in 1959, just as other makes followed its previous lead and moved it the other way! The intention was to beef up frontal appearance but all it did was make the machine look every pound of its not inconsiderable weight.

## Excelsior Monarch 1 (UK) 1959

Excelsior 147cc 2-stroke 8.4bhp engine
3-speed gearbox and 3.50 x 10 wheels
Maximum speed: 45mph/72kph
Weight: 300lb/136kg
Excelsior was keen to get its engine into the scooter market, but did not want to spend time designing its own frame and bodywork. A deal was negotiated with DKR to share that used for the Dove series. This was not very successful, especially when road performance and costs of the two machines were compared.

## Excelsior Monarch 2 (UK) 1962

Excelsior 147cc 2-stroke 8.4bhp engine
3-speed gearbox and 3.50 x 10 wheels
Maximum speed: 46mph/74kph
Weight: 249lb/109kg
When Excelsior did produce its own bodywork rather than borrowing DKR's, frontal appearance closely resembled that of the German Hercules and TWN Contessa. It was, however, not made of steel but fibreglass, and was designed to be quick-release for easy access to the engine. For those wanting better performance, Excelsior offered a larger capacity, 197cc Villiers engine.

## Excelsior Welbike (UK) 1941

Villiers 98cc 2-stroke engine
1-speed gearbox and 2.25 x 6.25 wheels
Maximum speed: unknown
Weight: 70lb/32kg

This wartime-designed machine was made by Excelsior for military use. It was designed to be folded and inserted into a tube and dropped by parachute to provide quick transport for invading armies. Side fuel tanks had to be pressurised by a hand pump before use. The peacetime version of the model was the Corgi.

## Ferbedo (West Germany) 1954

Zundapp 48cc 2-stroke 1.5bhp engine
2-speed gearbox and 2.75 x 8 wheels
Maximum speed: 25mph/40kph
Weight: 70lb/32kg

This basic scooter was advertised as an improvement on a pedal cycle. Normally, a wire cage covered the engine to protect hands from the hot and oily parts. It came with a rear-mounted luggage rack. There was a useful toolbox below the fuel tank. Colour choice was grey, red or green, and the scooter was on the market from 1954 until the end of 1955.

## Goggo 1 (West Germany) 1955

Goggo 150cc 2-stroke 5.5bhp engine
3-speed gearbox and 4.00 x 8 wheels
Maximum speed: 43mph/69kph
Weight: 242lb/110kg

This scooter was only briefly imported in the UK in 1954 by Cyclemaster to test the market. Gear changing was by left heel and toe foot pedals. It had an electric starter. It gave a very smooth ride but the importer considered it would not be price-competitive enough to sell well in the UK. In Germany the model was very successful. A stylish matching sidecar was available for the 197cc version.

## Goggo 2 (West Germany) 1956

Goggo 197cc 2-stroke 9.5bhp engine
4-speed gearbox and 4.00 x 10 wheels
Maximum speed: 53mph/85kph
Weight: 264lb/120kg
The front end of the previous model was restyled, giving it a heavier look, and braking was improved. There was a built-in engine inspection light under the dual seat. The Russians also made a version with the moniker of Tula, and also a three-wheel pickup version for commercial use which sold in large numbers throughout the USSR.

## Harley-Davidson Topper (USA) 1960

Harley-Davidson 165cc 2-stroke 9.5bhp engine
Auto gearbox and 4.00 x 12 wheels
Maximum speed: 46mph/75kph
Weight: 237lb/108kg
First appearing in 1960, the Topper came from the large, well-respected American motorcycle company of Harley-Davidson – which must have raised a few eyebrows. It had a pull cord starter, a fibreglass body and, unusually, was fitted with a parking brake. The enclosed engine did not have a cooling fan which, on occasion, led to overheating problems. The automatic drive was similar to that used in Europe by DKW. The last Toppers were produced in 1965.

## Harper Scootamobile (UK) 1954

Villiers 197cc 2-stroke 7.5bhp engine
3-speed gearbox and 4.0 x 12 wheels
Maximum speed: 55mph/88kph
Weight: 305lb/138kg
This was the British scooter that should have, but didn't, go into production as it was ahead of its time. The body was made of fibreglass. A smaller, 122cc engine was first tried but, as the scooter had a substantial, heavy frame, this was soon dropped in favour of the 197cc version. It had a car-type electric starter. Gear changing was via two foot pedals. Various prototypes incorporated different types of storage locker at the rear. Some early documents refer to the model as a Scootomobile.

## Heinkel Tourist A0 (West Germany) 1951

Heinkel 174cc 4-stroke 9.2bhp engine
4-speed gearbox and 4.00 x 10 wheels
Maximum speed: 55mph/90kph
Weight: 330lb/149kg

The Heinkel Tourist first arrived in the UK under the Excelsior brand name but, apart from the extra badges and British tyres, they were Heinkels. Soon, they were sold under this name but at a high retail price, restricting the number sold. The speedometer was fitted on the left in the pod below the handlebars, with a clockwork clock on the right-hand side.

## Heinkel Tourist A1 (West Germany) 1954

Heinkel 174cc 4-stroke 9.2bhp engine
4-speed gearbox and 4.00 x 10 wheels
Maximum speed: 55mph/90kph
Weight: 295lb/134kg

The A1 was probably the bestselling Heinkel model in the UK. It had a faultless electric starter system for which a backup kickstart was never necessary, but a less than perfect gearchange. This feature was never improved upon throughout the long life of the Heinkel Tourist; a shame, because the scooter was otherwise close to perfect in design. Today, it is possible to purchase a modern foot pedal modification.

## Heinkel Tourist A2 (West Germany) 1962

Heinkel 174cc 4-stroke 9.2bhp engine
4-speed gearbox and 4.00 x 10 wheels
Maximum speed: 55mph/90kph
Weight: 329lb/148kg

The shape of the rear end was revised to incorporate flashing indicators, which were also added to the front. Cast aluminium was provided for the footboard, which was rubber-mounted to prevent engine vibration. There was a useful tool storage space below the lockable large dualseat. In total around 180,000 Heinkel Tourists were produced. Engines continued in production until 1971 for the Greek Attica microcar.

## Heinkel 150 (West Germany) 1961

Heinkel 150cc 2-stroke 9bhp engine
3-speed gearbox and 3.50 x 10 wheels
Maximum speed: 53mph/85kph
Weight: 260lb/118kg
Heinkel had built a strong reputation on the four-stroke engine design, which was used in many thousands of Heinkel Tourist scooters and Kabincruiser bubblecars. It was surprising, therefore, that the Heinkel 150 was offered with a two-stroke engine in 1960. It was not a success and the last was built in 1965.

## Hirano Valmobile (Japan) 1961

Hirano 2-stroke engine
1-speed gearbox 4 inch wheels
Maximum speed: unknown
Weight: unknown
Little is known about this scooter except that it could be folded up, suitcase-size, and carried about! Similar machines from Europe and the USA hoped to tap into the market where a busy executive would store one in the boot of his car to use on shorter journeys from parking place to office. Regulations and restrictions meant they were not cost-effective, however.

## Iso Milano (Italy) 1959

Iso 146cc 2-stroke 6bhp engine
4-speed gearbox and 3.50 x 10 wheels
Maximum speed: 50mph/80kph
Weight: 215lb/98kg
A memorable magazine advert by Iso showed the Milano in motion, ridden by an attractive girl with a small dog peeking out of the side panel's bulge locker. The first Iso scooter, produced in 1948, had a small engine of 65cc and was of rather uninspired basic design. The Iso 150 Diva appeared in 1957, apparently a cross between a current Vespa and a Lambretta. The shape was a success and later it had faired-in handlebars and became known in the UK as the Iso Milano. The Iso company originated the Isetta bubblecar, and later went on to make high performance sports cars.

## Italjet Packaway (Italy) 1972

Italjet 49cc 2-stroke engine
Auto gearbox and 5 x 6 wheels
Maximum speed: 28mph-45kph
Weight: unknown

This was the original Corgi design brought up to date. The handlebars would fold inward and down across the fuel tank, and the seat could be lowered also. As with the Valmobile, the idea was that the little machine could be carried in a car boot and used for just a few miles in inner cities where parking is a problem. It could then be folded up and carried indoors.

## IWL Berlin (East Germany) 1963

IWL 143cc 2-stroke 7.5bhp engine
3-speed gearbox and 3.50 x 12 wheels
Maximum speed: 51mph/82kph
Weight: 297lbs/135kg

The first IWL scooter was produced in 1955 and was called the Pitty. The next model was the Wiesel in 1958, and the much more elegant Berlin was produced in 1959. This used some plastic and aluminium in its design. The Berlin was the most elegant Iron Curtain scooter, and offered a respectable performance with some style. The engine was developed from a DKW design which was copied by BSA for the Bantam motorcycle.

## IWL Pitty (East Germany) 1955

IWL 125cc 2-stroke 5.5bhp engine
3-speed gearbox and 3.50 x 12 wheels
Maximum speed: 45mph/75kph
Weight: 308lb/140kg

With the largest nose of any scooter, the Pitty was quite distinctive. It was not imported into the UK but did reach other overseas markets. The engine was developed from a DKW design and cooled by an electrically-powered fan, designed to cut in when the engine became hot. The Pitty was later developed into the more attractive Berlin. The word Pitty is an affectionate German version of the name Peter after the designer's son.

## IWL Troll (East Germany) 1964

IWL 150cc 2-stroke 9.5bhp engine
4-speed gearbox and 3.50 x 12 wheels
Maximum speed: 56mph/90kph
Weight: 282lb/128kg

After producing the Berlin scooter, the IWL company replaced it with what it considered was a more up-to-the-minute style, and the Troll is reminiscent of IWL's bestselling MZ utility motorcycle. The cylinder was cooled by a belt-driven fan, and a dash panel-mounted lamp indicated that the fan was still connected and doing its job. Aluminium and plastic were used, but still the machine was heavy for its capacity. Production ceased in 1966.

## James SC1 (UK) 1960

James 149cc 2-stroke 5.4bhp engine
3-speed gearbox and 3.50 x 12 wheels
Maximum speed: 53mph/85kph
Weight: 270lb/122kg

The first James scooter was rather late onto the market, but it did at least show some individuality in design. The horizontal engine was fitted under the footboard for a low centre of gravity. The central top cover lifted clear for accessibility. A good-sized storage area was therefore available under the seat for shopping, parcels and riding clothes. A mark 2 followed in 1963 with a 4-speed gearbox. Sadly, James closed down in 1966.

## Jawa Cezeta (Czechoslovakia) 1959

Jawa 175cc 2-stroke 8bhp engine
4-speed gearbox and 3.25 x 12 wheels
Maximum speed: 50mph/80kph
Weight: 286lb/130kg

1957 saw the first Cezeta using the standard motorcycle engine without extra cooling. The petrol tank was fitted above the front wheel with its filler cap behind the nose and headlamp. For the UK market the headlamp and horn changed places to comply with local regulations. The Cezeta had a push-in starting handle under the dualseat. It was also made under license in New Zealand where it was called the NZeta.

## Jawa Manet (Czechoslovakia) 1965

Jawa 98cc 2-stroke 5bhp engine
4-speed gearbox and 3.00 x 14 wheels
Maximum speed: 46mph/74kph
Weight: 243lb/110kg
Production continued from 1958 until 1969, by which time the Manet had become known as the Tatran S125 after receiving an alternative, 125cc, 7bhp engine in 1964. The sparkplug was accessible through an opening below the front of the seat. This was a reliable, well specified scooter with a built-in windscreen, indicators- and electric starter as standard.

## Lambretta A (Italy) 1948

Innocenti 125cc 2-stroke 4bhp engine
3-speed gearbox and 3.50 x 7 wheels
Maximum speed: 44mph/70kph
Weight: 154lb/70kg
The very first Lambretta scooter, the model A, was produced in 1947, the first of many hundreds of thousands that followed. It had a foot-operated gearchange, no rear suspension, concealed control cables and swept-back handlebars. This model was not imported into the UK, and the name Lambretta meant nothing here at that time. The similar-looking B model followed with a better suspension system and slightly larger 8 inch wheels.

## Lambretta C (Italy) 1950

Innocenti 125cc 2-stroke 4.3bhp engine
3-speed gearbox and 4.00 x 8 wheels
Maximum speed: 44mph/70kph
Weight: 154lb/70kg
The C had a tubular frame, hand gearchange, proper front and rear suspension, exposed cables, and a rod-controlled rear brake. The tyres were wider than before to give a softer ride. This model became the basis for the better-selling Lambrettas with side panels that followed, the first of which was the LC.

## Lambretta Cometa (Italy) 1968

Innocenti 74cc 2-stroke 5.2bhp engine
4-speed gearbox and 3.00 x 10 wheels
Maximum speed: 51mph/83kph
Weight: 170lb/77kg

The Cometa was almost identical to the Vega save for a separate oil tank, pump and injector for two-stroke fuel, a set-up which later became the norm for two-stroke scooters, but not readily accepted at the time. The Cometa was available in orange, turquoise, red, green and silver. Purchasers preferred to buy the cheaper Vega. The last Vegas and Cometas left the production line in 1970.

## Lambretta D (Italy) 1953

Innocenti 125cc 2-stroke 5bhp engine
3-speed gearbox and 4.00 x 8 wheels
Maximum speed: 44mph/70kph
Weight: 165lbs/75kg

Lack of rear bodywork kept production costs and purchase price low, and helped cool the engine, although all of those models which followed had bodywork. There was a demand then for an easy-to-clean, stylish look and Lambretta sales really took off! The D's engine had torsion bar suspension. There was a useful storage box behind the seat.

## Lambretta E (Italy) 1953

Innocenti 125cc 2-stroke 3.8bhp engine
3-speed gearbox and 4.00 x 8 wheels
Maximum speed: 44mph/70kph
Weight: 128lb/58kg

Starting was by way of an unreliable pull cord which gave many problems, so the next model – the F – had a normal kickstart instead. Few survive today in original condition, most having been converted to kickstart. A kit was later available to convert and improve the front suspension by fitting springs into the front forks.

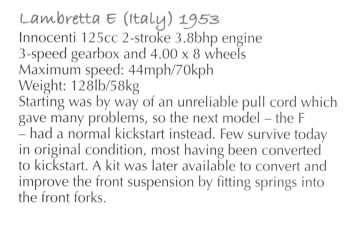

### Lambretta Eibar Li 150 (Spain) 1967

Eibar 148cc 2-stroke 6.5bhp engine
4-speed gearbox and 3.50 x 10 wheels
Maximum speed: 50mph/80kph
Weight: 254lb/105kg
Not sold in the UK, this was a Spanish-made version
with differences to the original Italian, one of which
was a front mudguard that rotated rather than being
fixed on the legshield. On the road performance was
similar to that of the Italian Li. This particular scooter
was displayed in the Kesterfield Collection in north
Devon and sold at auction following the death of
Mike Karslake, a great man and enthusiast who had
created the museum and preserved the memory of
Lambretta.

### Lambretta GP (Italy) 1970

Innocenti 150cc 2-stroke 9.2bhp engine
4-speed gearbox and 3.50 x 10 wheels
Maximum speed: 62mph/100kph
Weight: 265lb/120kg
This model was also available as a 125cc version.
In Italy the GP, or Grand Prix, was known as the DL
series. It had a rectangular headlight, and a slim body
style to reduce weight, production costs and air drag.
Plastic trimming changed from the previous grey
to black. The 125, strangely, sported a distinctive,
painted ink blot on the front right legshield ...

### Lambretta J 125 (Italy) 1966

Innocenti 125cc 2-stroke 5.8bhp engine
3-speed gearbox and 3.00 x 10 wheels
Maximum speed: 53mph/86kph
Weight: 198lb/90kg
This was a larger-engined version of the 98cc Cento
model. Earlier versions had two separate saddles,
whilst later ones had a dualseat. The design of the
kickstart was improved to make starting easier,
requiring less pressure and throw. It first appeared in
1964 and continued in production until 1966, when
it was superseded by the similar-looking Starstream
model.

## Lambretta LC (Italy) 1950
Innocenti 125cc 2-stroke 4.3bhp engine
3-speed gearbox and 4.00 x 8 wheels
Maximum speed: 40mph/65kph
Weight: 176lb/80kg
This was the first Lambretta to have bodywork. An
access door in the right side panel gave access to
the petrol tap and choke. Under the front saddle
was a small toolbox. The mechanics were exactly
the same as in the model C. In 1951 the LC was
replaced by the best-selling LD model, the first to
make an impression on – and subsequently flood
– the UK scooter market.

## Lambretta LD 1 (Italy) 1953
Innocenti 125cc 2-stroke 5bhp engine
3-speed gearbox and 4.00 x 8 wheels
Maximum speed: 44mph/70kph
Weight: 187lb/85kg
Externally, this model looked like the LC but used
the engine from the D. An Innocenti badge was fitted
above the headlamp. A fuel cap was fitted offset to
the right-hand side between the two separate saddles.
The kickstart pedal was the same shape as that
previously fitted on the LC model, and not as on the
D. Colour choice was grey or beige.

## Lambretta LD 2 (Italy) 1956
Innocenti 148cc 2-stroke 6bhp engine
3-speed gearbox and 4.00 x 8 wheels
Maximum speed: 46mph/75kph
Weight: 188lb/85kg
Grey rubber sleeves covered the control cables on the
handlebar, and the footboard runners were fitted with
rubber inserts. There was also a 125cc version that
did not have the rubber inserts in order to retail at a
lower price. The scooter shown here has been fitted
with a non-standard dualseat in place of the usual
two saddles.

## Lambretta LD 3 (Italy) 1957

Innocenti 125cc 2-stroke 5bhp engine
3-speed gearbox and 4.00 x 8 wheels
Maximum speed: 44mph/70kph
Weight: 198lb/90kg
The handlebars of the series 3 were improved by an aluminium cover. The rear numberplate was blended with the body, as was the rear light, giving a much smoother outline. A small lockable compartment was fitted into the body behind the rear saddle. The LDA version provided an electric starter. Demand often exceeded supply, as this was the scooter boom period in the UK. A 150cc version was also available.

## Lambretta Li 1 (Italy) 1958

Innocenti 125cc 2-stroke 5.2bhp engine
4-speed gearbox and 3.50 x 10 wheels
Maximum speed: 43mph/69kph
Weight: 229lb/104kg
The LI's rounded styling set the standard for scooters of the period. The front mudguard no longer turned with the steering. Wheel size increased from 8 to 10 inch. Drive was by duplex chain running in an oil bath rather than via the previous, relatively expensive shaft drive. A 150cc version was also available.

## Lambretta Li 2 (Italy) 1959

Innocenti 125cc 2-stroke 5.2bhp engine
4-speed gearbox and 3.50 x 10 wheels
Maximum speed: 43mph/69kph
Weight: 240lb/105kg
The main visual difference with the mark 2 was that the headlamp was taken from the legshield and placed onto the handlebars so that light was directed where the scooter was steering. This was a good and useful idea which also made the scooter appear sleeker and more dynamic. There was a wider choice of colours. This model further increased demand for Lambretta scooters and took the sales lead from Vespa in the UK.

## Lambretta Li 3 (Italy) 1965

Innocenti 148cc 2-stroke 6.6bhp engine
4-speed gearbox and 3.50 x 10 wheels
Maximum speed: 50mph/80kph
Weight: 254lb/105kg
The first of the Slimstyle bodies with narrower front profile. Although initially still designated an LI series, this model had quite a different modern, sleeker appearance. The speedo was rectangular and the headlamp had an octagonal rim. A battery was fitted as standard. The first examples were 125cc which, being cheaper to purchase, sold in greater numbers.

## Lambretta Rallymaster (Italy/UK) 1961

Innocenti 148cc 2-stroke 8.6bhp engine
4-speed gearbox and 3.50 x 10 wheels
Maximum speed: 50mph/80kph
Weight: 260lb/118kg
This was a special, UK-assembled and engine-tuned version of the Li for the sports rider, which incorporated a spotlight, a front tyre mud scrapper, ball-ended control levers, a rev counter, an illluminated rally board, and a clockwork stopwatch. It had lower gear ratios, and stood out from the crowd by virtue of the horizontal black stripes painted on the red sidepanels. The front mudguard did turn with the steering.

## Lambretta Starstream (Italy) 1966

Innocenti 122cc 2-stroke 5.8bhp engine
4-speed gearbox and 3.00 x 10 wheels
Maximum speed: 55mph/87kph
Weight: 198lb/90kg
A development of the former J series, the Starstream had slimmer styling with a larger dualseat. The engine also gave improved performance. Initially, the side panels were held on by turn levers but later models mirrored the larger Lambrettas in having spring clips instead. Production ceased in 1969.

## Lambretta Super Starstream (Italy) 1969

Innocenti 122cc 2-stroke 5.8bhp engine
4-speed gearbox and 3.00 x 10 wheels
Maximum speed: 55mph/87kph
Weight: 198lb/90kg
Side panels were held on by clips rather than a turning lever. Front suspension was improved. This model was produced in two-tone paintwork (red and white or blue and white). The front mudguard pivoted with the steering. This was the last, rarest and best of the J series Lambrettas.

## Lambretta SX 200 (Italy) 1966

Innocenti 198cc 2-stroke 11bhp engine
4-speed gearbox and 3.50 x 10 wheels
Maximum speed: 66mph/107kph
Weight: 271lb/123kg
The SX series was very identifiable by the forward-facing, arrow design of the side panel, and is one of the most powerful and sought-after Lambretta models today. It had a front disc brake; side panels were held on by spring clips rather than a turning handle. There was a square horn casing. It was also available in 125cc and a 150cc guises.

## Lambretta TV 175 1 (Italy) 1958

Innocenti 170cc 2-stroke 8.6bhp engine
4-speed gearbox and 3.50 x 10 wheels
Maximum speed: 64mph/103kph
Weight: 254lb/115kg
This model introduced a new, stylish body shape and offered, at least on paper, more power with a 4-speed gearbox. It suffered from many mechanical/engine problems, however, and did not perform as well as expected. The series 2 that followed scrapped the original TV engine in favour of an uprated version of the Li engine. The TV then took its rightful place as the most powerful Lambretta to date.

## Lambretta TV 175 2 (Italy) 1960

Innocenti 175cc 2-stroke 8.6bhp engine
4-speed gearbox and 3.50 x 10 wheels
Maximum speed: 55mph/90kph
Weight: 243lb/110kg

The TV 175 engine was developed from the more reliable Li series rather than the original TV series 1, which still had problems. The original TV was available in a cream colour only, but the series 2 could be had in blue and white or red and white. The headlamp was fitted onto the handlebars for much better illumination, just like the Li series.

## Lambretta Vega (Italy) 1971

Innocenti 74cc 2-stroke 5.2bhp engine
4-speed gearbox and 3.00 x 10 wheels
Maximum speed: 51mph/82kph
Weight: 168lb/76kg

Described as the Year 2000 scooter in 1968 when it first appeared, the Vega had a very individual, lightweight style. The engine was not covered though did have a cooling fan. The Cometa variant had a separate oil tank to obviate the need to mix petrol with oil at each fill-up. There was also a 50cc version called the Lui but this was not a UK import.

## Lamby Polo (India) 1987

API 150cc 2-stroke engine
4-speed gearbox and 3.50 x 10 wheels
Maximum speed: unknown
Weight: unknown

When Lambretta production ceased in Italy in the early 1970s, in 1973 it was restarted in India by the API company, which had bought the machine tools from Innocenti. Performance on the road was similar to the original Lambretta. A Japanese styling company was involved in updating the basic design, but whether or not the result was an improvement is debatable! The Indian factory had many labour and production problems, and supplies to the UK amounted to around only a dozen machines.

## Laverda 50 (Italy) 1960

Laverda 49cc 2-stroke 2bhp engine
2-speed gearbox and 2.50 x 9 wheels
Maximum speed: 32mph/52kph
Weight: 120lb/54kg

At first sight, the Laverda does not appear capable of much in the way of performance because of its tiny size. However, it did perform fairly well as its little engine was a four-stroke. Strangely, it had two silencers fitted on two exhaust pipes, one on each side of the scooter from the single cylinder engine. It was only available in an ivory colour. A 3-speed version followed and production continued until 1967.

## Laverda 60 (Italy) 1962

Laverda 60cc 2-stroke 3bhp engine
3-speed gearbox and 2.75 x 9 wheels
Maximum speed: 40mph/65kph
Weight: 139lb/63kg

This was the high performance Laverda! It was a bit of a joke really, and even the manufacturer had fun with it by producing a cowboy-style, tasselled seat cover. The body of the 60 was longer than that of the 50, and there was room for a spare wheel to be fitted horizontally behind the dualseat. In spite of its small size the little Laverda did achieve good results in some significant scooter road trials and long-distance runs.

## Maico Maicomobil (West Germany) 1959

Maico 197cc 2-stroke 10.3bhp engine
4-speed gearbox and 3.25 x 14 wheels
Maximum speed: 53mph/85kph
Weight: 250lb/114kg

1951 saw the introduction of this very individual machine; a scooter, but with many of the qualities of a conventional motorcycle: large wheels and the frame between the rider's legs. The large spare wheel is fitted across the rear of the twin side lockers. The fuel cap is sited on the dashboard. Bodywork is made from both steel and aluminium.

## Maico Maicoletta (West Germany) 1958

Maico 247cc 2-stroke 14bhp engine
4-speed gearbox and 3.25 x 14 wheels
Maximum speed: 65mph/105kph
Weight: 310lb/141kg
This magnificent scooter was almost perfect, but the 6 volt pendulum starter was the weak point in the design. If a kickstart had been provided – it was a heavy machine to push start – ownership would have been a total pleasure. Performance was satisying. Access to the fuel tap and air filter was through a hinged door on the left-hand side. The entire body easily lifted clear for maintenance. Originally known as the Comet, the Maicoletta was available from 1955 to 1964, and on special order from the factory until 1967.

## Manurhin Hobby (France) 1963

Manurhin 75cc 2-stroke 3bhp engine
Auto gearbox and 2.75 x 16 wheels
Maximum speed: 34mph/53kph
Weight: 176lb/80kg
The French-made, improved version of the German DKW Hobby. After DKW stopped making it in Germany, the scooter was further developed by getting a different carburettor and a fully automatic clutch to compliment the automatic gearchange. The last made examples were renamed Concorde. Today, automatic transmission on scooters is the norm but only the Manurhi offered this in Europe at the time.

## Mercury Hermes (UK) 1955

ILO 49cc 2-stroke engine
2-speed gearbox and 2.25 x 20 wheels
Maximum speed: unknown
Weight: 103lb/47kg
The Hermes was based on the German-made Meister Roller and, in Germany, was also available with a Sachs engine. Later versions of the Hermes had a Villiers engine in place of the imported ILO which was not well supported in the UK. The scooter later reappeared as the Dunkley Popular, with Dunkley's own small, 65cc, 4-stroke engine. Neither version sold well in the UK. Mercury also made two other scooters; the Dolphin and the Pippin.

## Mors-speed (France) 1951

Mors 115cc 2-stroke 3.8bhp engine
2-speed gearbox and 3.50 x 7 wheels
Maximum speed: 37mph/60kph
Weight: 132lb/60kg

This scooter was not sold in the UK but imported by a collector in recent years because of its novel design. It has a cast aluminium frame which incorporates the legshield. The gear change is controlled by two heel-operated pedals; one for up, the other for down. The last example was made in 1954. The follow-on machine was called the Paris Nice and was available in certain parts of the UK.

## Moto Guzzi Galletto (Italy) 1952

Moto Guzzi 192cc 4-stroke engine
4-speed gearbox and 3.00 x 17 wheels
Maximum speed: 53mph/85kph
Weight: 301lb/137kg

Locating the spare wheel vertically in front of the legshield was a unique design feature. The gear change was foot-operated by a single rocking pedal, and the footbrake was controlled by a heel-operated pedal sited on the left footboard. The big wheels gave the Galetto very good handling characteristics. It continued in production until 1966, appearing in the UK market at various times. Today, it is a very sought-after collectors' machine.

## Moto Rumi Little Ant (Italy) 1962

Moto Rumi 125cc 2-stroke 6.5bhp engine
4-speed gearbox and 4.00 x 8 wheels
Maximum speed: 46mph/75kph
Weight: 220lb/100kg

The Rumi Formichino scooter was available in three degrees of engine tune, all giving fine, spirited performance, comparable with machines of much larger capacity. The early models had a headlamp that turned with the steering inside the fixed housing. The engine formed the basis of the frame as the footboard and front and rear bodies bolted directly to it. Larger, 10 inch wheels and dual seats were later available.

## Motobecane Moby (France) 1957

Motobecane 150cc 2-stroke 5.2bhp engine
3-speed gearbox and 3.50 x 10 wheels
Maximum speed: 47mph/76kph
Weight: 216lb/98kg

This was based on the Motoconfort Utilitaire but with full bodywork and a larger engine (the two manufacturers were associated). The front suspension consisted of a concentric group of rubber bands, fitted under the mudguard. The rear was a large rubber block, supporting the rear of the pivoted engine. The fuel tank had a dipstick to check level, and on the opposite side was a storage locker.

## Motobecane SCC (France) 1954

Motobecane 125cc 4-stroke 5bhp engine
3-speed gearbox and 3.50 x 8 wheels
Maximum speed: 48mph/77kph
Weight: 209lb/95kg

First produced in 1951 the body was made of cast aluminium. Gear changing was by foot pedal, and the handlebar clutch and brake levers pivoted from their outside edge (the cables were concealed within the handlebar). It was a well-made, well-equipped scooter with individual style, but expensive to buy compared to the Italian imports. In 1954 it was replaced by a much cheaper, basic 2-stroke-engined scooter which did sell in larger numbers.

## Motobi Catria (Italy) 1959

Benelli 175cc 4-stroke engine
4-speed gearbox and 3.50 x 12 wheels
Maximum speed: 65mph/104kph
Weight: 275lb/125kg

The Catria scooter was developed from a motorcycle of the same name. It used the same engine and relied on cooling air passing through the tunnel on the footboard. The cylinder head was located at the front of the tunnel. Gear changing was via a right-hand side foot pedal. The last example was produced in 1962. A few of these models came to the UK but the later, large-wheeled Motobi Picnic model became better known. Motobi was a family offshoot of the larger Italian firm Moto Benelli.

## Motobi Picnic (Italy) 1959

Motobi 75cc 4-stroke 3.5bhp engine
3-speed gearbox and 2.50 x 16 wheels
Maximum speed: 43mph/70kph
Weight: 152lb/69kg

A forerunner of the large-wheeled step-through design so successfully developed later by the Japanese and which dominated the market in the mid-1960s; 100cc and 125cc 2-stroke engine versions were also produced  The same company also manufactured a more attractive and conventional-looking scooter called the Catria, small batches of which later became available in the UK.

## Motoconfort SB (France) 1956

Motoconfort 125cc 2-stroke engine
3-speed gearbox and 3.50 x 10 wheels
Maximum speed: 43mph/70kph
Weight: 165lb/76kg

This scooter was the French equivalent of the Lambretta D, having little bodywork and an open engine. Motoconfort was able to sell it for less than the Lambretta and it sold well in France. The fuel tank contained a removable dipstick with which to check fuel level. There was a carrier at the front and also one at the rear. The SB had fan cooling even though the engine was exposed; it wasn't sold in the UK.

## MV Agusta Chicco (Italy) 1961

MV Agusta 155cc 2-stroke 5.8bhp engine
4-speed gearbox and 3.50 x 10 wheels
Maximum speed: 53mph/85kph
Weight: 244lb/111kg

First produced in 1960, the Chicco was available until 1964. Its flowing styling was attractive. The foot controls were cast items; the small side panels restricted engine maintenance. If required, a second saddle could be affixed on top of the rear carrier. MV actually had plans for a 98cc motorcycle in 1945 to be called the MV Vespa, and four scooters were produced from 1945 to 1954 with similarities to the current Vespa, Lambretta, Iso and Parilla. It was to be five years before the more successful and better-known Chicco appeared.

## NSU Prima D (West Germany) 1957

NSU 147cc 2-stroke 6.2bhp engine
3-speed gearbox and 3.50 x 10 wheels
Maximum speed: 55mph/88kph
Weight: 270lb/123kg
NSU previously made the Lambretta Ld under licence, and in 1956 produced this very similar, improved 12 volt electric start scooter. It was well silenced, suspension was softer, and shock absorbers improved riding comfort. It was more upmarket than the original Lambretta with spare wheel, twin stands and a carrier as standard. It had an air of quality that did not transfer to its replacement in 1957.

## NSU Prima 3 KL (West Germany) 1959

NSU 174cc 2-stroke 9.3bhp engine
4-speed gearbox and 3.50 x 10 wheels
Maximum speed: 56mph/90kph
Weight: 304lb/138kg
Previously, NSU had successfully made the Prima D scooter derived from the Lambretta Ld it made under licence. This was NSU's first new design, which was not very successful, sales-wise. The engine had an unusual side action kickstart. A basic 150cc version was sold in Germany. The Deluxe version – called a V5 star – had a mudguard, fog light, and a clock on the dashboard.

## Oscar (UK) 1954

Villiers 197cc 2-stroke 8.4bhp engine
4-speed gearbox and 3.25 x 12 wheels
Maximum speed: 50mph/80kph
Weight: 275lb/125kg
This design had a fibreglass moulded body which did not leave much room for feet placement or foot pedal control of the gear change. It was also difficult to put a foot down onto the ground from the footboard. The foot brake controlled both brakes, front and rear. Only a few examples were made although a 125cc version was also advertised.

## Panther Princess (UK) 1959

Villiers 173cc 2-stroke 7.7bhp engine
4-speed gearbox and 3.50 x 10 wheels
Maximum speed: 53mph/85kph
Weight: 255lb/116kg

Not many examples were produced so this one is a very rare machine. Earlier Princesses were shown in the press with a square section front mudguard that turned with the front wheel, and with wider 4.00 x 10 tyres. The model shared some body panels with the Sun Wasp and Dayton Flamenco, but the front legshields gave it original style. It was advertised as available with either kickstart or electric starting. There was a neutral pilot lamp on the dash panel.

## Parilla Greyhound (Italy) 1957

Parilla 150cc 2-stroke 7bhp engine
4-speed gearbox and 3.00 x 12 wheels
Maximum speed: 52mph/85kph
Weight: 198lb/90kg

The Parilla first appeared in 1952 as a 125cc and sold well at home in Italy as well as in several overseas markets, including Germany and the USA. The design was the basis for Zundapp's later, even more successful, Bella scooter. The German Victoria Peggy resembled it also. UK sales weren't as good as those of the more popular Bella, which used disc rather than spoked wheels.

## Peugeot Elegant (France) 1957

Peugeot 147cc 2-stroke 6.6bhp engine
3-speed gearbox and 4.00 x 10 wheels
Maximum speed: 50mph/80kph
Weight: 250lb/113kg

The first version of this scooter – which appeared in 1953 – had a storage locker positioned above the front wheel. In 1957, the Elegant version was produced with a conventional front mudguard that followed the steering. (The original design became known as the Elite.) Around the same time the headlamp was moved up from the legshield to the handlebars. The bodywork could pivot up from the rear for engine access. Production ended in 1960 and did not resume until the recent past: Peugeot – now a major manufacturer – sells more scooters than ever before.

## Peugeot Elite (France) 1956

Peugeot 147cc 2-stroke 6.6bhp engine
3-speed gearbox and 4.00 x 10 wheels
Maximum speed: 50mph/80kph
Weight: 253lb/115kg

The slightly more expensive version of the Peugeot
Elegant scooter. Its only difference to that model is the
useful locker above the front wheel, on top of which
are runners to allow luggage to be carried. Two grab
handles were provided on the front legshield.
Early versions had 125cc engines and 8 inch wheels.

## Phoenix (UK) 1957

Villiers 147cc 2-stroke 6bhp engine
3-speed gearbox and 3.50 x 8 wheels
Maximum speed: 49mph/79kph
Weight: 195lb/119kg

Phoenix was a small company based in London
which produced a scooter capable of accommodating
a very wide range of Villiers single or twin engines.
At one time Phoenix advertised a 325cc model which
was then the largest capacity-engined scooter in the
world. Of simple design the original was basic in
the extreme, but did have a unique push down side
stand. The metal body was held on by pull to release
spring clips. Later versions used fibreglass bodies that
did display some style. Phoenix was never capable
of mass production so, although business continued
for several years (from 1956 to 1964), not a lot of
scooters were produced or are restored today.

## Phoenix (UK) 1959

Villiers 250cc 2-stroke 15bhp engine
4-speed gearbox and 3.50 x 10 wheels
Maximum speed: 70mph/112kph
Weight: 195lb/119kg

An easily removed plastic body gave good access to
the powerful twin fan-cooled engine. A 325cc version
was advertised though it is debatable whether it ever
made an appearance. This 250cc was probably the
largest capacity Phoenix seen on the road and could
be ordered as electric or kickstart. Like many British
manufacturers Phoenix took too long to sort out the
styling, by which time the market had contracted.

## Prior Viscount (West Germany) 1959

Sachs 191cc 2-stroke 10.2bhp engine
4-speed gearbox and 3.50 x 10 wheels
Maximum speed: 62mph/100kph
Weight: 316lb/143kg

Prior was the name eventually given to the imported German Hercules scooter. As there existed a British Hercules company which made bicycles, the name was changed for the UK to avoid confusion. When originally imported into the UK in 1955, however, the model was known under the importer's name of Keift. When Keift sold his business to concentrate on the production of DKR scooters (Day, Kieft and Robinson), the Hercules became known as the Prior.

## Progress Continental (West Germany) 1958

Sachs 191cc 2-stroke 10.2bhp engine
4-speed gearbox and 3.25 x 16 wheels
Maximum speed: 62mph/100kph
Weight: 305lb/139kg

Two Progress models were imported, and three made in the UK under licence with Villiers engines and fibreglass bodies. The British offerings were the 148cc Anglian, the kickstart 197cc Briton, and the electric start 197cc Britannia. The German-made continental model has an unusual legshield headlamp mounting that allows it to move with the steering; this feature was later dropped. A 147cc version was also available.

## Puch Alpine (Austria) 1960

Puch 147cc 2-stroke 6bhp engine
3-speed gearbox and 3.25 x 12 wheels
Maximum speed: 52mph/85kph
Weight: 282lb/128kg

The Alpine models first appeared in 1957. The SR had a kickstart whereas the SRL had an electric starter. A variant called the Puch Venus had a foot gearchange. (No connection with the Venus scooter.) The dualseat rises forward on a quadrant for access to the fuel cap. The body pivots at the front for engine access. A manual hand pump was fitted in the open behind the legshields. The follow-on models from 1960 were all of small capacity.

## Puch Cheetah (Austria) 1961

Puch 60cc 2-stroke 2.8bhp engine
3-speed gearbox and 3.00 x 12 wheels
Maximum speed: 37mph/60kph
Weight: 137lb/62kg

The Cheetah was still considered a scooter in spite of the position of the fuel tank between the rider's knees. The saddle was placed rather high, and could be a problem for some riders. Early versions had 50cc engines, but the 60cc version was more successful and eventually went on the power the more conventional follow-on model known as the Pony.

## Puch RL (Austria) 1954

Puch 121cc 2-stroke 4.5bhp engine
3-speed gearbox and 3.25 x 12 wheels
Maximum speed: 46mph/75kph
Weight: 180lb/82kg

This was Puch's first scooter, appearing on the market in 1952. The first models were not equipped with batteries but soon these R models were replaced by the RL which did have full facilities. The body was hinged at the front and could be lifted from the rear to access the engine. Another version had an extended frame for load carrying, either at the rear of or beside the scooter.

## Raleigh Roma (UK) 1961

Bianchi 78cc 2-stroke 4.5bhp engine
3-speed gearbox and 3.50 x 8 wheels
Maximum speed: 43mph/70kph
Weight: 172lb/78kg

The Roma was the Italian Bianchi Orsetto, or bear cub, scooter made under licence. Some plastic was used in the design. The footboards folded outward and the top cover lifted clear for easy access to the engine. Unusually, the dualseat could be positioned fore and aft to suit. Production continued until 1964 when Bianchi stopped making the Orsetto, and thus key parts for the Roma. It was also the end of the famous British bicycle company.

## Salsbury Motor Glide Aero (USA) 1937

Johnson 6.2cu in 4-stroke 0.75bhp engine
Auto gearbox and 3.50 x 6 wheels
Maximum speed: unknown
Weight: unknown
With rather amazing compact styling and simplicity, this design was brilliant for the late 1930s, and the model sold well in the USA long before scootering took off in Europe. The suspension system amounted to just low pressure tyres. The many available accessories included a large, rear-mounted bin to carry luggage. Smoother styling was gradually introduced in later years, which helped define the appearance of modern scooters.

## Servetta Lynx Royspeed (Spain/UK) 1983

Servetta 125cc 2-stroke 5.5bhp engine
4-speed gearbox and 3.50 x 10 wheels
Maximum speed: dependent on tuning
Weight: 264lb/120kg
Based on the Spanish-made Lambretta, this model was of a different era to the original, high performance Italian machines. Plastics were employed and changes made to lockers and controls. Various levels of UK tuning and modification were available to transform it into a much livelier performer. Lambretta was kept alive in Spain in the 1980s and in India up until the 1990s. Piaggio (Vespa) now owns the rights to the Lambretta name.

## Sim Ariete (Italy) 1953

Sim 148cc 2-stroke 7.5bhp engine
4-speed gearbox and 3.5 x 10 wheels
Maximum speed: 48mph/77kph
Weight: 176lb/80kg
In design the Ariete was rather like the open Lambretta D, in that it had a detachable rear body which covered the engine. It was available until 1955. Sim earlier produced a model in 1950 called the Moretti which used a three-speed Puch engine of 125cc. This had 8 inch wheels. A tunnel above the footboards channelled air to cool the engine. This model didn't come to the UK, but the same machine with a French engine called the Guiller was made under licence in Belgium. The last examples were made in 1958.

## Sun Geni (UK) 1958

Villiers 99cc 2-stroke 2.8bhp engine
2-speed gearbox and 2.50 x 15 wheels
Maximum speed: 37mph/60kph
Weight: 160lb/73kg

First produced in 1957, the Geni was an attempt
at a scooter without small wheels, a feature which
deterred many established motorcyclists. Conversely,
this lost it sales in the scooter enthusiast market as
many considered it wasn't a scooter if it had large
spoked wheels! By 1960, all usual Sun motorcycle
production had ceased, leaving only the Geni and
Wasp scooters. In 1961 the company was absorbed
by Raleigh.

## Sun Wasp (UK) 1959

Villiers 173cc 2-stroke 7.4bhp engine
3-speed gearbox and 3.50 x 10 wheels
Maximum speed: 50mph/80kph
Weight: 237lb/108kg

Sharing many body parts – and the same engine
– with the Dayton Flamenco, the Sun Wasp appeared
in 1959, although careful detailing created its own
style. It did have different electrics and gear change
system, however, with side-by-side foot pedals. The
shaped footboard design allowed easier contact with
the ground when stationary.

    The Italian word for wasp is Vespa; unfortunately,
the Sun model did not enjoy the same popularity as
the Italian Vespa.

## Swallow Gadabout (UK) 1947

Villiers 122cc 2-stroke engine
3-speed gearbox and 4 x 8.0 wheels
Maximum speed: 35mph/56kph
Weight: 202lb/91kg

Engine cooling was by way of air delivered via a
scoop below the footboard. Exhaust gases passed
to the rear via part of the frame. There was no
suspension. Gear changing was achieved by a lever
mounted on the left-hand side of the body. A Mk2
was introduced in 1949 which had a different, fan-
cooled Villiers engine and gear change by foot pedal.
A larger headlamp and a battery were fitted, as was
leading link front suspension. The rear part of the
bodywork hinged upward for easier access to the
engine. A commercial sidecar was made available.
The last example was produced in 1952.

## Tatran (Czechslovakia) 1966

Motokov 125cc 2-stroke 7bhp engine
4-speed gearbox and 3.00 x 14 wheels
Maximum speed: 50mph/80kph
Weight: 231lb/105kg
The Tatran name came about as the result of changes in the Czech motorcycle industry in the mid-1960s. The scooter is an updated and more powerful Jawa Manet which first appeared in 1958. A well specified machine with good riding qualities, it was exported to many other countries during its lifetime and gained a good reputation, continuing in production until 1969. Behind the scooter is a typical communist bloc PAV trailer, which was also used by microcars. Today, these trailers are much in demand and are being remanufactured in the UK.

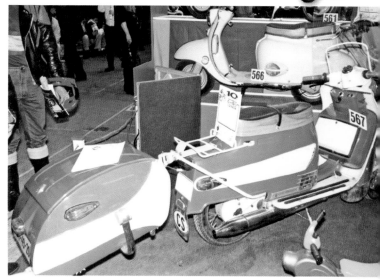

## Terrot (France) 1958

Terrot 125cc 2-stroke 5bhp engine
3-speed gearbox and 3.50 x 8 wheels
Maximum speed: 44mph/70kph
Weight: 200lb/91kg
As an option, the gears were pre-selectable by foot pedals, which allowed selection initially and engagement later when needed – all really rather unnecessary! Unusually, the handlebar levers pivoted from their outside ends. The scooter arrived in 1951 with a 98cc engine and only two speeds. In France, some Terrots appeared under the Magnet Debon name, an associated company. In spite of regular, good advertising in the UK, not many were sold here.

## Triumph Tigress (UK) 1960

Triumph 249cc 4-stroke 10bhp engine
4-speed gearbox and 3.50 x 10 wheels
Maximum speed: 63mph/101kph
Weight: 244lb/111kg
The Tigress was identical to the BSA Sunbeam apart from colour: the original choice in 1958 was green for BSA, blue for Triumph. The engine was a new design but the gearbox was derived from the Triumph Tiger Cub motorcycle. Engine choice was the same 175cc, 2-stroke alternative (derived from the BSA Bantam motorcycle). Production continued until 1964 for the twin and 1965 for the single.

## Triumph Tina (UK) 1963
Triumph 100cc 2-stroke 4.5bhp engine
Auto gearbox and 3.50 x 8 wheels
Maximum speed: 46mph/75kph
Weight: 163lb/74kg
The concept of a small-engined, fully automatic
scooter was a winning formula for the 1990s but,
sadly, not for the 1960s. The Tina arrived in 1962
but was plagued with mechanical problems due
to insufficient development. Originally, the front
mudguard was plastic but later became steel. The
footbrake being centrally mounted could be used
by either foot. It was replaced by the T10 in 1965
which was a more reliable development of the same
machine.

## Triumph T10 (UK) 1967
Triumph 100cc 2-stroke 4.5bhp engine
Auto gearbox and 3.50 x 8 wheels
Maximum speed: 46mph/75kph
Weight: 160lb/73kg
Developed from, and an improvement on, the
Tina, body shape was longer and more attractive.
Chromium-plating was used to brighten appearance.
The fuel cap was now located under the seat to avoid
soiling the rider's clothes. Build quality was not of the
highest standard, and electrical problems continued
so that many ran with safety cutouts disconnected.
The T10 continued in production until 1970.

## Triumph T10 Trike (UK) 1968
Triumph 100cc 2-stroke 4.5bhp engine
Auto gearbox and 3.50 x 8 wheels
Maximum speed: 43mph/70kph
Weight: unknown
A production run of just ten machines was undertaken
to test the UK market (similar tricycles had been
successful in Europe). A unique feature was that, on
bends, the front would lean while the rear remained
upright. It was decided not to proceed with full
production although the leaning technology was sold
to the Japanese who successfully used it on vehicles
such as the Honda Stream.

### Trobike (UK) 1961

Clinton 98cc 2-stroke 2.5bhp engine
1-speed gearbox and 3.50 x 5 wheels
Maximum speed: 30mph/48kph
Weight: 60lb/27kg
Originating from the company that imported
Lambretta scooters, the Trobike was a fun machine
that could be ordered in kit form with an engine
that came from an American lawnmower. The entire
machine could be carried in a microcar! The same
company also produced the Trojan Bubblecar.

### TWN Contessa (West Germany) 1957

TWN 197cc 2-stroke 10.4bhp engine
4-speed gearbox and 3.50 x 10 wheels
Maximum speed: 60mph/97kph
Weight: 328lb/149kg
This company was originally an offshoot from British
Triumph in the early 1900s, and used the Triumph
name in Germany. When the scooter was imported
to the UK in 1957, to avoid confusion as the design
was nothing to do with British Triumph, the title TWN
was used. The engine had two pistons within one
cylinder. Twin fuel tanks were located behind the
legshields. The same body and frame were used by
the Sachs-powered Hercules scooter. Puch of Austria
further developed the engine for its motorcycles.

### TWN Tessy (West Germany) 1957

TWN 150cc 2-stroke 7.5bhp engine
3-speed gearbox and 3.50 x 8 wheels
Maximum speed: 53mph/85kph
Weight: 228lb/104kg
Of really individual design and appearance, the Tessy
stood out from the crowd when it arrived in 1956.
The footboard tunnel ducted additional air to the fan-
cooled engine. Carriers were provided front and rear.
Sadly, production lasted for just one year, after which
the company concentrated on the larger Contessa. A
less powerful standard version, rated at 6bhp, was still
good for a 125cc.

## Unibus (UK) 1923

Precision 269cc 2-stroke engine
2-speed gearbox and 2.00 x 10 wheels
Maximum speed: 26mph/42kph
Weight: unknown

Considered by many to be the world's first ever production scooter with built-in weather protection, the Unibus was made in England by the Gloucester Aircraft Company. The engine was in the front, driving the rear wheel via a shaft. It was offered for sale at around £100 which, in the 1920s, was rather expensive for the mass market. Sadly, not many were sold. This was a landmark design in scootering. The same company produced a similar-looking, prototype 200cc scooter with larger 4.00 x 16 wheels as early as 1919.

## Velocette Viceroy (UK) 1961

Velocette 248cc 2-stroke 15bhp engine
4-speed gearbox and 4.00 x 12 wheels
Maximum speed: 70mph/113kph
Weight: 302lb/137kg

Development costs of the Viceroy was one reason why Velocette folded in 1971. The model had a brilliant. balanced twin cylinder engine design slung low and forward in the frame, but the rather ugly, massive styling turned off many perspective purchasers. The space available in the body was not used to any advantage, and the dash panel was poorly designed and crude-looking. Production ceased in 1964 with poor sales.

## Vespa 98 (Italy) 1947

Piaggio 98cc 2-stroke 3.3bhp engine
3-speed gearbox and 3.50 x 8 wheels
Maximum speed: 35mph/60kph
Weight: 198lb/90kg

The original Vespa outline, with the headlamp positioned on top of the front mudguard. Although many dismissed the design because of the offset location of the engine, which seemed to augur poor balance and possible instability, it was the start of great things to come. This same layout was used successfully for over 40 years.

## Vespa 125 (Italy) 1956

Piaggio 125cc 2-stroke 5bhp engine
3-speed gearbox and 3.50 x 8 wheels
Maximum speed: 47mph/77kph
Weight: 190lb/86kg

This model's simple, perfect styling captivated Europe and demand often exceeded the Italian factory's ability to supply. Many other factories were also producing the Vespa in other countries, including in the UK, where the old established firm of Douglas made them. For many years, Vespas became known as Douglas Vespas long after they were made in Italy only. A newspaper report of the time said "Britain to make Italian midget motorcycle", showing that the term 'scooter' had yet to be generally recognised.

## Vespa 90 SS (Italy) 1967

Piaggio 88cc 2-stroke 5bhp engine
4-speed gearbox and 3.50 x 10 wheels
Maximum speed: 55mph-88kph
Weight: 173lb-79kg

A real pocket rocket, the 90 SS had amazing performance for its engine size. Above the central spare wheel between the rider's legs was a glovebox (not a fuel tank as it appeared). It did offer promise of conventional motorcycle stability and control (to those who wanted this). The silencer had a motorcycle-type appearance.

## Vespa 180 SS (Italy) 1965

Piaggio 181cc 2-stroke 10.3bhp engine
4-speed gearbox and 3.50 x 10 wheels
Maximum speed: 63mph/101kph
Weight: 231lb/105kg

Beautiful, updated styling was combined with a more powerful engine than the 160cc GS model it replaced. The large locker behind the legshields was often converted by enthusiasts to house an onboard twin speaker audio music system (here was room for a larger battery to be fitted to supply the necessary power.) The 180 SS is considered by many to be the most beautiful-looking Vespa.

167

## Vespa Cosa (Italy) 1990

Piaggio 200cc 2-stroke 11bhp engine
4-speed gearbox and 4.00 x 10 wheels
Maximum speed: 62mph/100kph
Weight: 264lb/120kg

Many enthusiasts rejected this model as in 1985
Piaggio, the parent conmpany, wanted to move away
from the Vespa name and call it a Piaggio. A very
under-appreciated scooter with a rev counter and a
linked braking system, Plastic now appeared in the
design. It was no longer necessary to manually mix oil
with petrol as there was a separate tank and injector
system. Direction indicators were built in. The 125cc
and 150cc versions were dropped in 1990.

## Vespa GS (Italy) 1959

Piaggio 146cc 2-stroke 8bhp engine
4-speed gearbox and 3.50 x 10 wheels
Maximum speed: 62mph/100kph
Weight: 238lb/104kg

Many would claim this as the ultimate Vespa scooter.
It had 10 inch wheels when other Vespas had 8
inch versions, and was distinguished by its silver-
only finish. A stylish extra was a second circular
fuel tank that could be bolted behind the legshields.
Five versions appeared over as many years. It was
a legend in its own lifetime; a byword for style and
performance.

## Vespa GS Messerschmitt (West Germany) 1960

Piaggio 146cc 2-stroke 8bhp engine
4-speed gearbox and 3.50 x 10 wheels
Maximum speed: 62mph/100kph
Weight: 230lb/104kg

The best from two revered companies makes this a
real collectors' machine. Messerschmitt, of course,
is famous for its Kabinenroller bubblecars, but also
produced seven different Vespa models under license
up until the mid-1960s. Vespas were earlier produced
in Germany from 1949 until 1955 by the firm of
Hoffmann.

## Vespa Pedal 50 (Italy) 1973
Piaggio 49cc 2-stroke 1.4bhp engine
3-speed gearbox and 2.75 x 9 wheels
Maximum speed: 25mph/40kph
Weight: 145lb/66kg
Pedals were fitted to overcome government
regulations to allow those individuals licensed for
mopeds only to ride a Scooter. They were too heavy
to pedal far, but this offered a new market as a way
getting around the regulations! Pedal-less scooters
were still more popular where regulations didn't
require them.

## Vespa Rally 180 (Italy) 1971
Piaggio 181cc 2-stroke 10bhp engine
4-speed gearbox and 3.50 x 10 wheels
Maximum speed: 62mph/100kph
Weight: 218lb/103kg
An upgrade, with larger headlamp, to the 180 SS it
replaced, it was itself replaced within two years by
the more powerful 12bhp Rally 200. This was at a
time when scooter sales were declining worldwide,
owing largely to the increase in number, and lower
prices of, second-hand cars. Sporty scooters became
an increasingly important special interest area.

## Vespa Rally 200 (Italy) 1973
Piaggio 200cc 2-stroke 12bhp engine
4-speed gearbox and 3.50 x 10 wheels
Maximum speed: 65mph/105kph
Weight: 218lb/103kg
Building on the success of the 180 Rally, the 200
offered a little more power with 12bhp, and a higher
top speed. Body styling went unchanged except for a
white band painted along the side panels. Electronic
ignition followed which vastly improved acceleration
and reliability. Production continued until 1977.

## Vespa Rod Model (Italy) 1950

Piaggio 125cc 2-stroke 5bhp engine
3-speed gearbox and 3.50 x 8 wheels
Maximum speed: 44mph/70kph
Weight: 195lb/89kg

This model was so named because of the gear change control linkage system from the handlebar. To comply with UK regulations, the headlamp was now sited near the top of the legshield. This was the scooter that first had a noticeable presence on the UK's roads, offering – for the first time – comfortable and economic personal transport. A square rubber pad could be fixed on top of the luggage carrier for a passenger to sit on.

## Vespa Sportique (Italy) 1962

Piaggio 145cc 2-stroke 5bhp engine
4-speed gearbox and 3.50 x 10 wheels
Maximum speed: 51mph/82kph
Weight: 189lb/86kg

A popular special version of the Sportique was called the Supreme, which had many extras for little extra cost. Model names often varied, depending on which country it came from and which it was marketed in. To meet the demand that local production could not, Vespas were imported from other countries, albeit sometimes only briefly.

## Vespa T5 (Italy) 1987

Piaggio 123cc 2-stroke engine
4-speed gearbox and 3.50 x 10 wheels
Maximum speed: 65mph/104kph
Weight: 227lb/103kg

In terms of performance the T5 achieved a high level. The dashboard information was excellent. At the time of writing, the two-stroke T5 is being phased out of production owing to new regulations regarding air pollution. Although not of the usually accepted classic period, the model deserves a mention here; it is certainly a true milestone in scooter evolution and is remembered with affection.

## Victoria Nicky (West Germany) 1955

Victoria 48cc 2-stroke 2.5bhp engine
2-speed gearbox and 2.25 x 20 wheels
Maximum speed: 34mph/55kph
Weight: 132lb/60kg

Very few of these small, single-saddle scooters were sold in the UK, although its German manufacturer claims to have sold 200,000 of the engines to sixty different countries. There was a starting handle rather than a kickstart, and panelling over the top of the engine, situated between the footboards, could be lifted clear for maintenance purposes. Under the saddle was a convenient storage compartment for tools which could be locked. The rear section of the body was an aluminium casting.

## Vjatka V150M (Russia) 1955

Vjatka 150cc 2-stroke 5.5bhp engine
3-speed gearbox and 4.00 x 10 wheels
Maximum speed: 44mph/70kph
Weight: 266lb/110kg

I was amazed to come across one of these scooters – virtually a direct copy of the Vespa GS – in a street whilst visiting Moscow in 1964. In those days there was no way a western scooter could have been imported. It clearly carried a Vjatka badge, although no agreement had been made with Piaggio to make it there under licence. A 175cc version was to follow in the 1960s. It continued in production well into the 1980s.

## Wabo (The Netherlands) 1958

Villiers 147cc 2-stroke 6bhp engine
3-speed gearbox and 3.00 x 14 wheels
Maximum speed: 50mph/80kph
Weight: unknown

One of those rare occasions when an overseas company decided it would import British Villiers engines to power its own design of scooter; usually, it was Germany that benefited from such trade. The Wabo was really just an enclosed light motorcycle, imported exclusively by one dealer, Claude Rye of London, and sold mostly via regular adverts in weekly motorcycle magazines. A 98cc 2-speed version was also available.

## Zundapp Bella R 150 (West Germany) 1954

Zundapp 150cc 2-stroke 7bhp engine
4-speed gearbox and 3.50 x 10 wheels
Maximum speed: 50mph/80kph
Weight: 259lb/118kg

Zundapp entered the scooter market quite early, and decided to develop a design based on the Italian Parilla Greyhound which had been selling well in Italy. Zundapp's conventional motorcycle engine could be fitted without the need for fan cooling, as air was ducted over the engine through the central tunnel. The fuel cap was fitted under the side-lifting rear seat. Rubber-cushioned foot pads were fitted into the cast aluminium footboards.

## Zundapp Bella R 204 (West Germany) 1958

Zundapp 198cc 2-stroke 12.4bhp engine
4-speed gearbox and 3.50 x 10 wheels
Maximum speed: 55mph/90kph
Weight: 306lb/139kg

The rear number plate mounting incorporated a useful storage area for the supplied tool kit. Bella scooter sales exceeded those of Zundapp motorcycles. Good and regular sales in the UK were later frustrated as the importer Ambassador decided to replace the Bella with its own design, which was not a success. A year later Ambassador re-imported the Bella. It was one of the best German scooters, and sales exceeded those of the Italian Parilla, the basis for its design.

## Zundapp R 50 (West Germany) 1964

Zundapp 49cc 2-stroke 2.9bhp engine
3-speed gearbox and 3.50 x 10 wheels
Maximum speed: unknown
Weight: unknown

The last Zundapp scooter model to use a small engine, taken from the Falconette moped. A higher-performing engine of 4.6bhp with a 4-speed gearbox was fitted on the RS 50 version. An 80cc model also became available. This scooter did not come to the UK but did continue in production for many years. The Zundapp factory closed in 1985. Much of the production machinery was sold to China.

# Microcars

### AC Petite (UK) 1955
Villiers 346cc 2-stroke 7.75bhp engine
3-speed gearbox and 2 seats
Maximum speed: 49mph/80kph
Weight: 870lb/395kg
This little car was first produced in 1953 by a company which had enjoyed considerable success in the early 1900s with three-wheeler economy cars. The rear-mounted engine in the Petite was rather noisy, and tended to easily overheat, causing clutch problems. The engine drove the gearbox via a V-belt and the final drive to the rear differential was by chain. Later models had a 353cc, two-stroke engine. Much later the same company produced the famous AC Cobra.

### AC Town Car (UK) 1971
Puch 500cc 4-stroke engine
Auto gearbox and 2 seats
Maximum speed: unknown
Weight: unknown
When production of Villiers engines declined, AC turned to Austria for a supply of suitable engines. This car was a prototype testing the fitment of one of those engines. The Town Car could have been a competitor for Reliant but only three were ever made. AC became the UK's largest producer of government-financed specialist economy cars for invalids which used Puch engines.

### Acoma Comtesse (France) 1981
Motobecane 49cc 2-stroke engine
Auto gearbox and 2 seats
Maximum speed: unknown
Weight: unknown
Thanks to French regulations it was easy and cheap for basic economy cars with small engines to take to the road, and many companies flourished as a result, with Acoma one of the largest manufacturers. Fibreglass bodywork was used because of its light weight. The engine and fuel tank are behind the front fold-out bonnet. Front and rear suspension was by coiled springs.

## Aixam (France) 1999

Lombardini 500cc diesel engine
4-speed gearbox and 4 seats
Maximum speed: unknown
Weight: unknown

Sales of modern microcars in the UK began to increase in the late 1990s, especially after the demise of the local Reliant three-wheeler company, whereupon many ex-Reliant dealers sold the Aixam instead. The model offered advantages to those who did not hold a full car driving licence. Other economical engines are available. The same company also make V12 Supertrucks.

## Arola (France) 1977

Sachs 47cc 2-stroke 3bhp engine
Auto gearbox and 2 seats
Maximum speed: 25mph/40kph
Weight: 230lb/110kg

Arola was another big name in French microcar production; again, using fibreglass bodies fitted with small motorcycle engines, which also helped keep purchase price low. Arola's first such car was produced in 1976, with doors made of transparent plastic sheet. Another version had a pick-up load area for light loads. There were three- and four-wheel versions. After the initial boom sales declined and the company closed in 1983.

## Autobianchi Bianchina 110 (Italy) 1962

Fiat 499cc 4-stroke 21bhp engine
4-speed gearbox and 4 seats
Maximum speed: 55mph/90kph
Weight: 1190lb/540kg

The Italian Fiat group was the creator of many interesting small cars and variants. Autobianchi was expert at modifying the more mainstream Fiat small cars and turning them into eye-catching and attractive alternatives. There were also two-seater and cabriolet versions of this attractive little car.

## Autobianchi Bianchina Coupé (Italy) 1957

Fiat 479cc 4-stroke 16.5bhp engine
4-speed gearbox and 2 seats
Maximum speed: 55mph/90kph
Weight: 1078lb/490kg

The Bianchina was based on the Fiat 500 platform but was a much better appointed car. It had a roll-top canvas roof, and a 500cc, unrated engine was used in place of the original from 1958. Production continued until the mid-1960s. This model had a higher retail than the original Fiat but fulfilled the wish of many to have something different and sporty, at least in appearance.

## Bamby (UK) 1984

Suzuki 49cc 2-stroke engine
Auto gearbox and 1 seat
Maximum speed: 37mph/60kph
Weight: 235lb/107kg

A retry of the Peel microcar idea which, sadly, did not sell in any quantity. The engine came from a current Suzuki moped. The Bamby could be legally driven on just a moped licence so the market could have been a large one. It gave full weather protection and had motorcycle running costs.

## Berkeley B90 (UK) 1959

Royal Enfield 492cc 4-stroke 30bhp engine
4-speed gearbox and 2 seats
Maximum speed: 66mph/106kph
Weight: 718lb/326kg

40bhp and 50bhp versions of the B90 were produced, using engines from the Royal Enfield motorcycle though, very often, owners later fittted alternative engines. This particular example has a relatively modern Honda engine. Berkeley also produced miniature caravans, and even a double-decker caravan, but sales of these declined rapidly, leaving many unsold and leading to company closure in 1960.

## Berkeley T60 (UK) 1959

Excelsior 328cc 2-stroke 4.2bhp engine
4-speed gearbox and 2 seats
Maximum speed: 60mph/97kph
Weight: 718lb/326kg

Available in three- and four-wheeler form, the Berkeley was another design from Laurie Bond, who designed the Bond Minicar. Light bodywork made the most of engine performance. With all-round independent suspension, the T60 was a miniature sports car. The three-wheeled version sold rather better than the four- as it cost less to buy and run. A modern version has been remade and is available in kit form.

## Berkeley Mini (UK) 1962

BMC 848cc 4-stroke 34bhp engine
4-speed gearbox and 2 seats
Maximum speed: 70mph/113kph
Weight: unknown

Towards the end of Berkeley production, and even afterward, many conversions were carried out on the T60 in an effort to increase performance and visual appeal. The wheelarches were extended and some bonnet extensions made so that the Mini engine unit and front suspension could be fitted. This version has some extra cooling air intake holes along the top edge of the front grille, and exit vents ahead of the doors.

## Biscuter (Spain) 1955

Hispano Villiers 197cc 2-stroke 6bhp engine
4-speed gearbox and 2 seats
Maximum speed: 52mph/85kph
Weight: 528lb/240kg

The British engine company Villiers had an agreement with the Spanish Hispano company to make several of its engines under license. These led to the local design and production of several different microcars, of which the Biscuter was the most successful. The engine had a cylinder head twice the width of the cylinder to assist with cooling, as there wasn't a cooling fan. Coupé and commercial versions were available.

## BMW Isetta (West Germany/UK) 1959

BMW 295cc 4-stroke 13bhp engine
4-speed gearbox and 2 seats
Maximum speed: 50mph/80kph
Weight: 792lb/360kg

Isettas were also made in the UK at this time in order to satisfy demand during the peak period for microcar sales. It was possible to buy a new microcar for less than the cost of a second-hand conventional car. The name Isetta originated from the Italian word for little Iso, the name of the Italian company that originally designed and made them. Dependent on different country road tax regulations, one or two closely spaced wheels were fitted at the rear. The steering column moves forward away from the driver as the door opens for ease of entry.

## BMW Isetta Pick-up (West Germany) 1959

BMW 295cc 4-stroke 13bhp engine
4-speed gearbox and 2 seats
Maximum speed: 50mph/80kph
Weight: 803lb/365kg

Although this version has a soft top for the load area, an option for the Isetta Pick-up was a solid roof luggage area with a lockable door, and many of these were used by the German Post Office. There was also a full, low-level open pick-up version with four normally spaced wheels, made by the Italian Iso company.

## BMW 600 (West Germany) 1959

BMW 582cc 4-stroke 19.5bhp engine
4-speed gearbox and 4 seats
Maximum speed: 62mph/100kph
Weight: 1245lb/565kg

Longer than the original Isetta, the 600 could carry a total of four passengers (two more than the Isetta) and so, in 1957, appealed to a much wider market. It continued in production for two years. There was a right-hand, side-opening passenger door at the rear. Many loyal owners of the original bubblecars bought a 600 as their family increased, and it became unofficially known as the Isetta 600.

## BMW 700 (West Germany) 1961

BMW 697cc 4-stroke 30bhp engine
4-speed gearbox and 4 seats
Maximum speed: 77mph/125kph
Weight: 1410lb/640kg

Developed from Isetta 600 mechanics and with the body designed by Micheloti, the 700 took the BMW image more upmarket. This car was produced for six years, with great appeal for the driver wanting a more sporting look. It was available as a saloon and as a coupé. Sales of this car allowed BMW to invest profits in the design of much more powerful and profitable cars for the future.

## BMW 700 Sport (West Germany) 1961

BMW 697cc 4-stroke 40bhp engine
4-speed gearbox and 2 seats
Maximum speed: 83mph/135kph
Weight: 1507lb/684kg

Appearing in 1962, a tuned engine and suspension improvements gave an enhanced ride and better performance. Although specified as a four-seater, in truth, there was very little space for more than two people, a situation later improved by increasing wheelbase length and reducing the padding used in front seat backrests.

## Bond Bug (UK) 1972

Reliant 700cc 4-stroke 29bhp engine
4-speed gearbox and 2 seats
Maximum speed: 75mph-120kph
Weight: 874lb/396kg

The Bug was designed by Ogle and built by Reliant, which had just taken over the Bond company. The Reliant engine was increased in size in 1973 to 750cc at 31bhp. It was a very individual, futuristic design that stood out from the crowd, available only in orange: a classic seventies statement. Although small-engined microcars were no more in the UK, the Bug proclaimed a future for three-wheelers. It was last made in 1974 after 2268 Bugs had been produced as Reliant decided to put all of its resources into production of the new Robin.

## Bond Minicar B (UK) 1952

Villiers 197cc 2-stroke 8.4bhp engine
3-speed gearbox and 2 seats
Maximum speed: 50mph/80kph
Weight: 420lb/190kg

This little car was one of the first to appeal to those who could not afford to buy or run a conventional car; so much so that the factory had to be expanded in order to meet demand. Laurie Bond was the man who went on to design many other microcars. Later versions of the Bond Minicar, although still bearing his name, were not designed by him but by Sharps Commercials, the company that produced them. The Mark B resembled the prototype Mark A.

## Bond Minicar D (UK) 1958

Villiers 197cc 2-stroke 8bhp engine
3-speed gearbox and 4 seats
Maximum speed: 50mph/80kph
Weight: 470lb/213kg

The Bond Mark D – which resembled the Mark C – and all later Minicar models could turn around completely within their own length as the engine unit turns with the steering mechanism. Quite a unique feature which meant the car could be driven into a dead end and out again without needing to reverse (so reverse gear wasn't required). This same idea was tried on an earlier Pashley microcar but that had larger wheels which restricted its turning circle. The Mark D was also available as a saloon and a two-seater.

## Bond Minicar F (UK) 1959

Villiers 246cc 2-stroke 11.5bhp engine
4-speed gearbox and 4 seats
Maximum speed: 52mph/85kph
Weight: 672lb/305kg

Available also as a two-seater, a coupé and a van, the Mark F was manufactured from 1958. It had a rather odd appearance as the long, flat-sided body sat on small, eight inch diameter wheels. The larger engine gave it more power than the previous E model, although sales were not as good. It was replaced in 1961 by the improved and larger-wheeled Mark G Minicar.

## Bond Minicar G Coupé (UK) 1963

Villiers 250cc 2-stroke 11.5bhp engine
4-speed gearbox and 2 seats
Maximum speed: 53mph/85kph
Weight: unknown

Known as the Tourer, this was the last of all the
various models of Bond Minicar. Production
continued for more than ten years, during which time
over 26,000 Bond Minicars were produced. The Mini
name had been introduced to the world of motoring
ahead of the more famous Morris Mini. The Bond
name continued on the larger-engined 875, and later
into the 1970s with the Bug, even though, by then,
the company had been taken over by Reliant. This
poor quality picture does not show the car at its best,
unfortunately.

## Bond Minicar G Estate (UK) 1963

Villiers 250cc 2-stroke 11.5bhp engine
4-speed gearbox and 4 seats
Maximum speed: 52mph/84kph
Weight: 856lb/388kg

Like the saloon, the estate was available with
a single or a twin engine (the twin was quieter
and smoother in operation). Interior space was
generous for a microcar. A pull-open sunroof was
available. There was a lifting hatchback, which
made the car very accommodating for many
uses, and the back seat could be folded forward
to increase load area. It was also available as a
commercial van, complete with blanked-out side
windows. Production continued until 1966.

## Bond Minicar G Saloon (UK) 1962

Villiers 250cc 2-stroke 11.5bhp engine
4-speed gearbox and 4 seats
Maximum speed: 52mph/84kph
Weight: 856lb/388kg

The most characteristic features of the G saloon were
the larger wheels and treatment of the rear window,
which swept inward at the base (a design also seen
then on the Ford Anglia). Which company was first
to use that design is hotly debated. The brakes were
hydraulically operated and the windows wound up
rather than slid, as in conventional cars. The Minicar
had also become longer than some regular cars!

## Bond 875 (UK) 1966

Rootes 875cc 4-stroke 34bhp engine
4-speed gearbox and 4 seats
Maximum speed: 82mph/132kph
Weight: 896lb/407kg

When the Bond Minicar ceased production in 1966, the company decided to produce a more powerful three-wheeler, thereby giving would-be purchasers of the Reliant a more attractive alternative. The Hillman Imp van engine gave the fibreglass-bodied car perhaps too much power for safety, and steering was not of the highest order. The 875 was also produced as a van at an even lower price than the saloon. In 1969 the company was absorbed by Reliant and production came to a halt soon after.

## BSA Ladybird (UK) 1960

BSA 249cc 4-stroke 10bhp engine
4-speed gearbox and 2 seats
Maximum speed: 63mph/101kph
Weight: unknown

The Ladybird used the engine from the BSA Sunbeam scooter. It had handlebar steering, no roof, and a pull lever for the starter as an alternative to the electric one. It did not have a windscreen wiper. Only two prototypes were made, and it is believed that only one remains. This was BSA's attempt to make its own microcar with which to challenge the bubblecars from Germany. In the end, the company decided that it could not compete in terms of production costs, and concluded that an open car would not sell so well in the UK. The Ladybird's body shape very closely resembled that of the German Tourette microcar.

## Coronet (UK) 1958

Excelsior 328cc 2-stroke 18bhp engine
4-speed gearbox and 4 seats
Maximum speed: 55mph/90kph
Weight: 810lb/368kg

The Coronet used suspension and steering mechanics from the Standard 8 motor car. Like most similar vehicles, it had a body made from fibreglass and, in appearance, resembled the aluminium-bodied Powerdrive microcar, but with smoother lines. It was intended to have standard car space with better economy. Production continued for about two years.

## Cursor (UK) 1986

Suzuki 49cc 2-stroke engine
Auto gearbox and 1 seat
Maximum speed: 30mph/48kph
Weight: unknown
The Cursor was designed to comply with the government's definition of a moped so that virtually anyone could drive it with minimum qualification from the age of sixteen. The engine was mounted in the middle of the fibreglass body. A slightly more powerful two-seater version with gull wing doors was available later but no more than fifty were made in total.

## Decsa Lisa (San Morino) 1984

123cc 2-stroke engine
Auto gearbox and 2 seats
Maximum speed: unknown
Weight: 715lb/325kg
This attractive little microcar was made in San Marino, Europe's smallest country, and was engineered and sold by the French Lambretta company. The air-cooled engine was mounted at the rear of the fibreglass body. This is very likely the only example that exists in the UK, imported for its novelty value, and seen at microcar rallies in recent times. It is believed that the same San Marino company also produced three-wheeler microcars.

## Erad (France) 1980

290cc diesel engine
4-speed gearbox and 2 seats
Maximum speed: unknown
Weight: unknown
Seen at a national microcar rally, little is known about this intriguing little car, other than that it comes from another of France's "Voiture sans Permis" manufacturers. Regulations placed maximum weight and speed restrictions on these vehicles. Although lacking in performance, they were very economic to buy and run. Erad has made a wide range of such cars for many years using petrol and diesel engines that have varied in size from around 50 to 500 cubic centimetres.

### Ercomobile (Switzerland) 1999

BMW 4-stroke various engines
4-speed gearbox and 2 seats
Maximum speed: 100mph/161kph
Weight: dependent on engine
This fantastic vehicle has two main wheels, with two side stabiliser wheels that touch down at low speeds. It is built to order in Switzerland, commanding a very high price. In spite of that, many have found enthusiastic buyers who can specify the level of performance required. Driver and passenger sit in tandem. The Ercomobile is quite a sight to see in motion as it leans over at speed when cornering. It was designed by Arnold Wagner, an airline pilot.

### Felber TL400 (Austria) 1954

Rotax 398cc 2-stroke 16bhp engine
4-speed gearbox and 2 seats
Maximum speed: 51mph/82kph
Weight: 1188lb/540kg
Felber of Austria was a sidecar manufacturer that decided to manufacture and sell a microcar. In 1953, it produced the first model: an open three-wheeler with a 350cc Rotax engine in the boot and just one headlamp. Produced in 1954, the Felber was the next model – and the last. As with the original model, it also had a single front seat, and the rear twin engine drove the single rear wheel. There was now a fabric hood for weather protection, plus front wings and two headlamps. A more durable add-on roof section later became available. The vehicle did perform well enough to win awards in some sporting events.

### Fiat 126 (Italy) 1976

Fiat 594cc 4-stroke 25bhp engine
4-speed gearbox and 4 seats
Maximum speed: 57mph/92kph
Weight: 1130lb/514kg
Although not strictly microcars, this book includes small cars that regularly attend microcar rallies, which the Baby Fiats do so whilst Minis don't (probably because the Fiats have smaller engine capacity and they are relatively rare in this country). The Fiat 126 was a 1976 replacement for the Fiat 500, with more modern angular styling and a little more space inside and in the boot. In 1987 production moved from Italy to Poland, when it was known as the 126 Bis. It eventually received a water-cooled engine in place of the original air-cooled unit.

## Fiat 500 F (Italy) 1965

Fiat 499cc 4-stroke 18bhp engine
4-speed gearbox and 4 seats
Maximum speed: 55mph/90kph
Weight: 1106lb/502kg

First made in 1957, the Fiat 500 set the standard for the small economy car, although there was very little space at the rear or in the front boot, which also contained the fuel tank. Previous to this F model from 1965, the 'suicide' doors opened from the front, now considered unsafe. The car also received a larger windscreen for better driver visibility, and more power for the engine. It was a very popular car in Italy and around the world. Today, Fiat is about to release a modern small car which closely resembles the F's classic shape and styling.

## Fiat 500 Special (Italy) 1973

Fiat 479cc 4-stroke 16.5bhp engine
4-speed gearbox and 4 seats
Maximum speed: 55mph/90kph
Weight: dependent on version

This Special is symbolic of the multitude of open and variant versions of the Fiat 500 – buggies, sportsters, racers, estates – produced between 1957 and 1975 by many different firms, including Autobianchi, Abarth, Ghia, Moretti, and Vignale under licence from Fiat. Other companies in other countries modified the little car.

## Fiat 600 (Italy) 1956

Fiat 633cc 4-stroke 22bhp engine
4-speed gearbox and 4 seats
Maximum speed: 59mph/95kph
Weight: 1260lb/572kg

The 600 followed on in 1955 from the prewar-designed Fiat Topolino as Fiat's main small car. It was quiet and water-cooled; a feature of the design was elimination of greasing points. In 1960, the D model arrived with a larger 767cc engine. The doors now had front end hinges. Opening quarterlight windows and bumper overriders also featured.

## Fiat Gamine (Italy) 1967

Fiat 499cc 4-stroke 18bhp engine
4-speed gearbox and 2 seats
Maximum speed: 55mph/90kph
Weight: unknown

Based on the rear-engined Fiat 500 F, the Gamine was produced by the Vignale company from 1967 until 1969. The front radiator was simply an impressive styling exercise, reminiscent of earlier Lancias, which gave the little car individuality and a new image. A folding hood helped with weather protection.

## Fiat Giardiniera (Italy) 1971

Fiat 499cc 2-stroke 18bhp engine
4-speed gearbox and 4 seats
Maximum speed: 55mph/90kph
Weight: 1232lb/559kg

This was an estate version of the Fiat 500. The engine was inclined to reduce height and give more useful space at the rear of the car. Initially produced by Fiat from 1960, production transferred to Autobianchi in 1965. The rear door opened sideways. Factory publicity for the car used the American term, Station Wagon; a rather grand title for such a small car.

## Fiat Multipla (Italy) 1958

Fiat 767cc 2-stroke 32bhp engine
4-speed gearbox and 6 seats
Maximum speed: 55mph/90kph
Weight: 1276lbs/580kg

First produced in 1956, the Multipla was based on the Fiat 600. The spare wheel fitted inside the car below the dashboard. It was the first true People Carrier as we understand the term today; that is, a car which will accommodate more than four people (it could carry six). In recent years, Fiat has reintroduced the name for another unique, forward-thinking design with the same objective.

## FMR Messerschmitt KR175
### (West Germany) 1954

Sachs 174cc 2-stroke 9bhp engine
4-speed gearbox and 2 seats
Maximum speed: 56mph/90kph
Weight: 462lb/210kg

The Fend pedal-driven invalid car was developed into the motor-driven Fend Flitzer with a twistgrip for the throttle, and cable-operated brakes. A large spring sited under the seat served as a shock absorber! The passenger sat behind the driver. The Messerschmitt KR175 was a further development of the Flitzer. The car had the Messerschmitt name because that company invested in it, worked with Fend to improve the design, and then built it in the Messerschmitt factory.

## FMR Messerschmitt KR200
### (West Germany) 1960

Sachs 191cc 2-stroke 9.7bhp engine
4-speed gearbox and 2 seats
Maximum speed: 62mph/100kph
Weight: 528lb/240kg

In 1955 the Messerschmitt received standard car controls except for a curved steering handlebar. Shock absorbers were fitted and the larger engine gave it an excellent power-to-weight ratio. Body styling was slightly revised to achieve good aerodynamics with low drag. All gears were available in reverse because the engine was simply stopped and restarted to rotate in the opposite direction. The KR200 became a class-leading bubblecar, its Perspex dome giving rise to the name and used for other, similar vehicles. In Germany it was known as a Cabin Scooter.

## FMR Messerschmitt KR200 Cabrio
### (West Germany) 1960

Sachs 191cc 2-stroke 9.7bhp engine
4-speed gearbox and 2 seats
Maximum speed: 64mph/103kph
Weight: 495lb/225kg

Instead of the usual plastic bubble dome, the Cabrio had a fabric soft-top above framed side windows. Very often as the car aged, any problems with the expensive and difficult-to-fit dome resulted in it being removed and replaced by a fabric soft-top. Although originally more dome-tops than Cabrios were sold, because of this problem, soft-top Cabrios are now more common.

## FMR Messerschmitt KR201 (West Germany) 1961

Sachs 191cc 2-stroke 9.7bhp engine
4-speed gearbox and 2 seats
Maximum speed: 64mph/103kph
Weight: 466lb/212kg

This sporty version had no fixed side windows but a folding canvas hood with side curtains, and also a shaped, lower height windscreen. This was the roadster model that originally sold for less than the other models. A significant event in Messerschmitt history occurred when Mercedes objected to flying bird design of the original badge, which could have been mistaken for its star symbol. The initials FMR were then used on the nose of all Messerschmitts in place of the bird symbol. In English this translates to Regensberg machine factory.

## FMR Lastenroller (West Germany) 1962

Sachs 191cc 2-stroke 9.7bhp engine
4-speed gearbox and 1 seat
Maximum speed: 62mph/100kph
Weight: unknown

Keen to develop a new sales market toward the end of production of the Messerschmitt bubblecar, the same engine was used in a lightweight tricycle for local delivery work. There were variations in body design and materials; wood and steel was used to suit different loads. Sales were moderately good and a Mark 2 version followed.

## FMR Messerschmitt Mini Tiger (West Germany) 1959

BMC 998cc 4-stroke 55bhp engine
4-speed gearbox and 2 seats
Maximum speed: 80mph/128kph
Weight: unknown

Pushing performance limits, this car was modified in Switzerland by fitting a Mini engine, done because spares for the original FMR engine were unobtainable at the time. With the availability of newly-manufactured spares, the car has since been converted back to original condition in engine and bodywork. It was, however, a very intriguing, good-performing design which deserved to be preserved. Sadly, a standard Tiger commands a higher price!

## FMR Messerschmitt Record Breaker (West Germany) 1955

Sachs 191cc 2-stroke 9.7bhp engine
4-speed gearbox and 1 seat
Maximum speed: 77mph/125kph
Weight: 506lb/230kg including 60kg of ballast
A modern replica of the special Messerschmitt microcar that set 25 records for performance and endurance at the German Hockenheim race track in 1955. Ballast was added to equal the weight of a standard Messerschmitt. It ran for 24 hours at an average speed of 65mph (105kph), including six driver changes and refuelling. It achieved a maximum speed of 77mph (125kph). One of the drivers was Fritz Fend, who designed the Messerschmitt.

## FMR Messerschmitt Sport (West Germany) 1960

Sachs 191cc 2-stroke 9.7bhp engine
4-speed gearbox and 2 seats
Maximum speed: 64mph/103kph
Weight: 466lb/212kg
This model didn't have an opening door; the driver had to climb over the padded side. It had a very low Perspex windscreen and a flat tonneau cover, and actually cost more to buy than the other models, but did not sell as well. To drive this car safely goggles were needed, and, on other than a dry day, full, foul-weather kit, too. It did, however, have a very sporty image.

## FMR Messerschmitt Tiger (West Germany) 1959

FMR 493cc 2-stroke 20bhp engine
4-speed gearbox and 2 seats
Maximum speed: 80mph/130kph
Weight: 770lb/350kg
Developed by FMR, this ultimate Schmitt has excellent performance and superb style, with two rear wheels in place of the usual one, and a much more powerful engine. In its day, performance was close to that of the then sporting version of the Morris Mini. I was a co-driver in the 1963 Esso 'Scoot to Scotland Edinburgh Run' event where three Tigers won the Class award in competition with a team of BMC Minis.

## FMR Messerschmitt Tiger Cabriolet (West Germany) 1959

FMR 493cc 2-stroke 20bhp engine
4-speed gearbox and 2 seats
Maximum speed: 80mph/130kph
Weight: 748lb/340kg

Like the Messerschmitt KR200 bubblecar, the Tiger could be converted to a soft-top Cabrio, so pleasant to drive on a fine day. Some Tigers have been converted to avoid problems with a damaged Perspex dome; others to resemble the KR200 Sport which, with no side window frames and only a short windscreen, provides more sporty motoring.

## Fuldamobile N1 (West Germany) 1951

Baker Polling 247cc 2-stroke 8.5bhp engine
3-speed gearbox and 2 seats
Maximum speed: 46mph/75kph
Weight: 1056lb/480kg

This little car had a wooden frame and bodywork. This is the only example left of what was a big-selling, famous range of microcars which was eventually made under licence in several different countries, often with different names. Fuldamobile began microcar production in Sweden in 1950. The owner was Karl Schmitt; no connection whatsoever with the other famous microcar which has come to be affectionately known as a 'Schmitt'.

## Fuldamobile S1 (West Germany) 1955

ILO 197cc 2-stroke 9.5bhp engine
3-speed gearbox and 4 seats
Maximum speed: 50mph/80kph
Weight: 1155lb/525kg

This car had an aluminium body. Production was left in the hands of another company – NWF – as the original factory did not have sufficient capacity to meet microcar demand. Later, this design was also made in the UK as the Nobel when it had a fibreglass body sourced from Bristol Aircraft Ltd, and a 191cc, 2-stroke Sachs engine. The S1 was also made in Greece with a 200cc, 4-stroke Heinkel engine, where it was known as the Attica.

### Funtech 50 (France) 2001

Morini 49cc 2-stroke engine
Auto gearbox and 2 seats
Maximum speed: 43mph/69kph
Weight: unknown

This fun microcar can also be classified as a moped
so may be driven by sixteen year-olds if they can
afford the insurance! It can be supplied with a
fixed tow bar for towing behind a motorhome, thus
providing convenient transport from a camping site.
It is available in blue, yellow and red. Body panels
are made of plastic. A canvas roof and doors are also
available.

### Funtech 350 (France) 2001

Lombardini 338cc 4-stroke engine
Auto gearbox and 2 seats
Maximum speed: 50mph/80kph
Weight: 444lb/202kg

This version has more power and an extra wheel, but
a full license is required to drive it. There is a useful-
size, lockable boot behind the plastic seats. Front and
side bull bars and a rear carrier are also available. A
targa roof kit can be purchased to keep off the rain,
but it's most fun in the sun! Insurance costs are high
for this vehicle, which has limited sales.

### Goggomobile 400 Coupé (West Germany) 1961

Glas 395cc 2-stroke 20bhp engine
4-speed gearbox and 2 seats
Maximum speed: 60mph/96kph
Weight: 950lb/431kg

This Goggomobile had rear-mounted, twin cylinder,
air-cooled engines. The front bonnet did not open
as it served only to cover the footwell. A semi-
automatic gearbox could be specified; a clutch-only
gear change. Early examples had suicide doors which
opened from the front. In the Coupé rear seating was
only suitable to carry luggage.

## Goggomobile T250 (West Germany) 1957

Glas 245cc 2-stroke 13.6bhp engine
4-speed gearbox and 4 seats
Maximum speed: 50mph/80kph
Weight: 851lb/386kg

The Goggomobile – being a four-wheeler – was discriminated against in the UK as it attracted the same rate of road tax as a standard car, whereas the rate for three-wheeled microcars was very much lower. This was not the case in Germany where the Goggomobile became the most successful and best-selling microcar. Its design was not revolutionary – it was essentially just an inexpensive small car with a small engine – but this was the secret of its success.

## Goggomobile T400 (West Germany) 1959

Glas 395cc 2-stroke 20bhp engine
4-speed gearbox and 4 seats
Maximum speed: 62mph/100kph
Weight: 1014lb/460kg

The best-selling version of the Goggomobile; around a quarter of a million were produced, which gives an indication of just how important the microcar market was in the late 1950s. Unfortunately, the higher UK tax band for four-wheeled cars was detrimental to sales. The Goggo name originated from the pet name given to the designer's nephew and was first given to the company's scooters.

## Goggomobile TL400 (West Germany) 1959

Glas 395cc 2-stroke 20bhp engine
4-speed gearbox and 1 seat
Maximum speed: 59mph/94kph
Weight: 1320lb/600kg

This van version was used by many small businesses in Europe, including the German Post Office. A relatively high roof meant it could carry quite bulky loads, though it still managed to perform well for its small engine size, and look attractive. It was also available as an open-topped pick-up.

## Goggomobile TS300 Cabriolet (West Germany) 1958

Glas 293cc 2-stroke 14.8bhp engine
4-speed gearbox and 2 seats
Maximum speed: 56mph/90kph
Weight: 915lb/415kg

Manufactured by the Glas company, Goggomobiles first appeared in 1955 and continued in production until 1969 when taken over by BMW. Unlike a lot of microcars, the Goggomobile was designed from the start to carry four people. Engine sizes were 247cc, 296cc and 400cc. Glas held the world record for the highest number of microcars produced and sold.

## Gordon (UK) 1955

Villiers 197cc 2-stroke 8bhp engine
3-speed gearbox and 2 seats
Maximum speed: 50mph/80kph
Weight: 700lb/318kg

The Gordon came about as the result of an investment by the then-famous Vernons Football Pools company when, in 1954, it hoped to produce the cheapest possible practical two-seater car to buy and run. The small engine – curiously, located where you would expect to find the driver's door – did not need fan cooling in this exposed position so no power was wasted in that direction. Three wheels also promised better economy (it was capable of achieving over 60mpg). It sold until 1958 when production ended.

## Heinkel (West Germany/Ireland) 1957

Heinkel 174cc 4-stroke 9.2bhp engine
4-speed gearbox and 4 seats
Maximum speed: 53mph/86kph
Weight: 535lb/243kg

The Heinkel had the ideal bubble shape, and was designed to accommodate another, smaller bench seat behind the front one, accessible by folding down the front backrest and stepping over the seat. A larger, 198cc engine followed in 1957. There were patent problems with BMW over the Isetta, so, to avoid this, production was stopped in Germany and transferred to Ireland, where the car was badged as a Heinkel Ireland. In 1961 production switched to England and the car became known as the Trojan Cabin Cruiser.

## Honda N600 (Japan) 1973

Honda 598cc 4-stroke 40bhp engine
4-speed gearbox and 4 seats
Maximum speed: 75mph/120kph
Weight: unknown

An automatic version was also available which was
revolutionary for a small car. This, based on Honda's
N360 microcar, was the first Honda car to be sold
in the USA, which became a major market. It is
interesting to remember that Honda made its first car
as late as 1962 but now is one of the world's giants.
Previously known only for its motorcycles, Honda
now has an American factory also.

## Honda Z Coupé (Japan) 1971

Honda 598cc 4-stroke 40bhp engine
4-speed gearbox and 2 seats
Maximum speed: 75mph/120kph
Weight: 1680lb/764kg

The Z Coupé was based on the N600 saloon,
but had a lower, shorter, more stylish and sporty-
looking body which allowed it to achieve higher
speeds. Disc brakes were fitted and the rear
window opened to stow luggage on the small
back seat (which was all it was suitable for).

## Inter (France) 1956

Ydral 175cc 2-stroke 8.5bhp engine
3-speed gearbox and 2 seats
Maximum speed: 50mph/80kph
Weight: 374lb/170kg

Curiously, the front suspension could be folded
inward when the car was not being driven, which
meant less storage space! The passenger sat behind
the driver and the roof opened sideways in a similar
manner to the Messerschmitt. The engine was at the
rear. Note the single front headlamp. The model –
which had a very individual style – was first produced
in 1953 and continued until 1956.

## Isard 400 Coupé (West Germany) 1959

Glas 395cc 2-stroke 20bhp engine
4-speed gearbox and 2 seats
Maximum speed: 60mph/96kph
Weight: 950lb/431kg

The Goggomobile name was changed to Isard when
it was offered for sale in France, so this is really a
Goggomobile by any other name. A saloon was
also available but the Coupé was the sporty version,
available in a range of two-tone colours. The doors
hinged at the rear, so care was needed opening them
in following traffic.

## King Midget Mark 3 (USA) 1967

Kohler 476cc 4-stroke 12bhp engine
Auto gearbox and 2 seats
Maximum speed: 50mph/80kph
Weight: 670lb/304kg

This American microcar briefly came to the UK in
1997 as part of the Bruce Weiner microcar collection
auction at Christie's. That auction, by the way,
produced world records for prices paid for classic
microcars, with buyers from North America, Europe
and Japan. King Midget produced microcars for over
twenty years in the USA. The first Midgets, which
had independent suspension, were sold as home-
constructed kits in 1949, but were not available in the
UK.

## Kleinschnittger (West Germany) 1954

Ilo 123cc 2-stroke 6bhp engine
3-speed gearbox and 2 seats
Maximum speed: 43mph/70kph
Weight: 330lb/150kg

Suspension was provided by rubber bands, front
and rear. The body was quite small and made of
lightweight aluminium; some scooters were heavier! It
was front-wheel-drive with no reverse gear, and fitted
with very recognisable and characteristic wheel discs.
The fuel tank was also tiny, with a capacity of just 1.5
gallons. The car was available from 1950 until 1957.

## Lambretta Mink (UK) 1968

Innocenti 198cc 2-stroke 11bhp engine
4-speed gearbox and 2 seats
Maximum speed: 60mph/96kph
Weight: unknown

The UK Lambretta importer experimented with the idea of producing a microcar using a Lambretta engine. This was the prototype but production did not follow because, it is believed, handling was not good due to the long frontal overhang. The front two wheels were located halfway along the body: there was no way its road manners could be significantly improved with such a design.

## Lightburn Zeta Sports (Austalia) 1964

FMR 493cc 2-stroke 20bhp engine
4-speed gearbox and 2 seats
Maximum speed: 75mph/120kph
Weight: 896lb/407kg

A stock of surplus German FMR Tiger engines was discovered by one of the original British Frisky design team, and he hoped to design a car to take them. The result was the Lightburn Zeta Sports, financed and put into production in Australia. The chassis was a modified version of the one fitted in the Frisky Sport. There was also a saloon model Zeta (which bore no resemblance to the Sport version), that used a Villiers 324cc engine, as had the Frisky. A pick-up joined the range, too. Production of all models had ended by 1967.

## Ligier (France) 1999

Lombardini 500cc diesel engine
4-speed gearbox and 2 seats
Maximum speed: 55mph/88kph
Weight: 761lb/346kg

The Ligier was one of several new microcars to appear in the UK in the late 1990s and was imported by the firm that had previously made the Reliant. It was quite cute in appearance, but the driving experience was not good. One TV motoring program presenter abandoned the car in mid-test, saying he couldn't continue! A range of alternative small engines was offered, automatic and manual.

## Lloyd 650 (UK) 1949

Lloyd 654cc 2-stroke 17.5bhp engine
3-speed gearbox and 2 seats
Maximum speed: 46mph/74kph
Weight: 1344lb/515kg

Lloyd was a small British company with no connection to the better-known German firm of the same name, with a factory in Grimsby. Lloyd had been producing interesting small cars, engines and transmission designs since the 1930s. The 650 saw the light of day in 1946. The engine was a water-cooled, two-stroke twin with front-wheel-drive. It had an early form of fuel injection and all-round, independent suspension. With its many forward-thinking features, it cost more to buy than the average conventional car so sales were not large. Production ceased in 1951. The company then continued for another 30 years or so doing specialist work for other companies in the car industry.

## Lloyd Alexander (West Germany) 1958

Lloyd 597cc 4-stroke 25bhp engine
4-speed gearbox and 4 seats
Maximum speed: 62mph/100kph
Weight: 1243lb/565kg

Lloyd cars came from the same company that produced Borgward and Goliath. They began production in 1950 with small-engined, wooden-bodied cars, with large wheels. By 1958, Lloyd was producing metal-bodied cars though still with small engines. The product was intended to target the market gap just above microcars but ceased production in 1961 as conventional cars became cheaper. The company was taken over by the Audi Group.

## Meadows Frisky (UK) 1958

Villiers 324cc 2-stroke 16bhp engine
4-speed gearbox and 2 seats
Maximum speed: 60mph/97kph
Weight: 715lb/325kg

This was the original, practical four-wheel version of the Frisky, an earlier design that was not proceeded with which had gull-wing doors. Its larger engine gave it better performance, but a higher road tax had to be paid as a result. An open-topped sports version was also available. Although the Frisky had four seats, those at the rear were only suitable for small children. Production stopped in 1961 in order to concentrate on the more popular three-wheeler.

## Meadows Frisky Family Three (UK) 1962

Villiers 197cc 2-stroke 9bhp engine
4-speed gearbox and 2 seats
Maximum speed: 50mph/80kph
Weight: 672lb/305kg

Meadows liked the microcar design of an ex-army engineer who had intended to produce the car in Egypt, where he thought there would be a large market. That never happened, but in the UK manufacture and sales got off to an encouraging start in spite of the fact that four wheels levied higher taxes. Soon, the three-wheel version arrived, becoming the best-selling Frisky. It was a stylish-looking car with a fibreglass body; main drawbacks were that it had very little headroom and rear hinging doors. A 250cc engine was also available. Production continued until 1964

## Meadows Frisky Sport (UK) 1959

Villiers 324cc 2-stroke 18bhp engine
4-speed gearbox and 2 seats
Maximum speed: 65mph/104kph
Weight: 700lb/318kg

This two-seater version was also known as the Roadster. The alternative Coupé could have a hard-top or a soft-top. Again, the doors pivoted at the rear and the catches were sometimes unreliable. There were chromium overriders but no bumpers. In the last year before the company closed there were hopes of good sales of a larger-bodied model called the Prince, but fewer than ten were produced.

## Microcar MC1 (France) 2005

Lombardini 505cc 4-stroke 21bhp engine
Auto gearbox and 4 seats
Maximum speed: 72mph/116kph
Weight: 781lb/355kg

A luxury model with 8-spoke alloy wheels and a transparent roof. Sales have been very satisfactory in the UK as the model offers, for the first time, a real alternative to the class-leading Smart with the added advantage that its light weight allows it to be driven on a motorcycle licence. Available also as a two-seater with a shorter body, the lack of rear seats gives a large luggage space.

## Microcar Virgo (France) 1999

Lombardini 505cc 4-stroke engine
4-speed gearbox and 2 seats
Maximum speed: 60mph/100kph
Weight: unknown

A modern French microcar employing the famous
alloy, direct injection, Lombardini water-cooled,
two-cylinder, four-stroke engine used by many other
modern microcars. The body is made from fibreglass
and is mounted on a steel frame. There is a full height
rear door with low-loading facility. The rear seats are
only suitable for small children or luggage.

## Mikrus (Poland) 1959

WSK 293cc 2-stroke 14.8bhp engine
4-speed gearbox and 4 seats
Maximum speed: 56mph/90kph
Weight: 990lb/450kg

Observing the success of the Goggomobile in the
west, communist Poland decided to virtually copy
it. Production started in 1956 and continued slowly
until around 1700 cars had been produced in three
years. There were cabriolet and pick-up prototypes,
but none went into production. The model suffered
from unreliability and overheating in summer months,
neither was build quality the best and so very few
survive.

## Mochet Velocar (France) 1951

Ydral 125cc 2-stroke 5bhp engine
3-speed gearbox and 2 seats
Maximum speed: 30mph/48kph
Weight: 528lb/240kg

This company was founded in the 1920s, and
specialised in small-engined economy cars, some of
which had engines of just 100cc. In France, these
cars benefited from fewer regulations. Originally,
this model had spoked wheels, giving it a very old-
fashioned appearance. It had cable brakes and chain
drive, and leaf springs at the rear.

## Mopetta (West Germany) 1957

DKW 49cc 2-stroke 2.3bhp engine
2-speed gearbox and 1 seat
Maximum speed: 29mph/45kph
Weight: 134lb/61kg

The little vehicle was made by Brutsch, part of the Opel group. Only fourteen examples were ever made; the sales potential for individual, small, cheap, independent personal travel had appeared larger than it actually was! The Mopetta's designer had previously made larger microcars, including the beautiful Spatz. This one was only 67 inches (170cm) long, an attribute that the Sinclair C5 hoped to capitalise on in later years, but with similar results.

## Nobel 200 (UK) 1960

Sachs 191cc 2-stroke 9.7bhp engine
4-speed gearbox and 4 seats
Maximum speed: 58mph/93kph
Weight: 660lb/300kg

The British version of the German Fuldamobile. The plastic body came from Bristol Aircraft Ltd, which had a department specialising in making aircraft fuel tanks. The car was assembled by Short Brothers in Northern Ireland, and used the same engine as the Messerschmitt. Here, the driver and passenger sat side-by-side and, as a consequence, the car was noticeably slower on the road than the Messerschmitt. The Nobel was available also as a pick-up and a self-build kit.

## Nobel Pick-up (UK) 1962

Sachs 191cc 2-stroke 9.7bhp engine
4-speed gearbox and 1 seat
Maximum speed: 60mph/96kph
Weight: unknown

This was an interesting commercial variant of the Nobel 200, which appeared in the last year of that models' production based on the Fuldamobile S-7T (which enjoyed considerable success in Germany, surviving until 1969). The floor and engine cover was made of plywood. The cable-operated brakes were not the most efficient and the wheels were small. Carrying heavy loads was not the Pick-up's fabvourite occupation, but bulky, light ones were quite acceptable.

## NSU Prinz 2 (West Germany) 1959

NSU 583cc 4-stroke 26bhp engine
4-speed gearbox and 4 seats
Maximum speed: 64mph/105kph
Weight: 1092lb/496kg
This two-cylinder, air-cooled, rear-engined car
had all-round independent suspension. The spare
wheel was carried in the front boot. A tuned 36bhp
engine became available from 1960. The model was
superseded by the larger Prinz 4 in 1962. In 1969,
NSU merged with Audi and the marque disappeared,
having been a leader for some years in scooter and
small car production.

## NSU Sport Prinz (West Germany) 1962

NSU 583cc 4-stroke 30bhp engine
4-speed gearbox and 2 seats
Maximum speed: 80mph/130kph
Weight: unknown
This car had a completely different image and
appearance to the Prinz saloon. With bodywork
designed by Bertone, improved aerodynamics
resulted in a livelier and faster feel and performance.
This body shape was later developed to house NSU's
famous Wankel rotary engine in the 1964 Spider (see
following entry). In that form the car could achieve
nearly 100mph (160kph). Today, the Wankel engine
lives on, in development and production by the
Japanese Mazda car company.

## NSU Wankel Spider (West Germany) 1965

NSU 500cc Wankel 64bhp engine
4-speed gearbox and 2 seats
Maximum speed: 96mph/155kph
Weight: 1540lb/700kg
This was the car that first used the newly-developed
revolutionary Wankel rotary engine. Unfortunately,
the engine was not as successful as was expected, and
later versions of the Spider used a more conventional
engine design to avoid the many reliability problems
experienced with the Wankel. Mazda of Japan later
bought the rights to the engine design and still uses
modern versions of it.

## Opperman Unicar (UK) 1957

Excelsior 328cc 2-stroke 18bhp engine
4-speed gearbox and 2 seats
Maximum speed: 58mph/95kph
Weight: 700lb/318kg
The Unicar – which was designed by Laurie Bond – could be ordered ready-assembled or as a do-it-yourself kit, when it would have been delivered by post in eight parcels. The fibreglass body housed the engine in the sealed boot, and access to it was via the back seat. There was no opening front bonnet, although there was a useful, large front shelf under the dashboard. A development in 1958 was the larger Stirling with a more stylish, swept-back style. It has been claimed that production of this car was halted by big names in the car industry who put pressure on parts suppliers.

## Paul Vallee Cockerel (France) 1957

Ydral 125cc 2-stroke 5bhp engine
3-speed gearbox and 2 seats
Maximum speed: 46mph/74kph
Weight: unknown
In French the name is Chantecler. With a fibreglass body, and a canvas roof that could be rolled open, the Cockerel was built for just two years – 1957 and 1958 – which serves to illustrate how tenuous was the life of many microcars at that time and why surviving examples are rare; only two are known to exist. The same firm also produced some very interesting motor scooters; none of which were UK imports either.

## Peel P50 (UK) 1962

DKW 49cc 2-stroke 4.2bhp engine
3-speed gearbox and 1 seat
Maximum speed: 30mph/48kph
Weight: 132lb/60kg
The only car to be made in the Isle of Man, the P50 was the smallest-roofed car in the world. The engine was located behind the front right-hand wheel. To reverse the car, the driver has to get out and pull it round by a grab handle at the rear! The fibreglass body had just enough room inside for one occupant. The wheel arrangement on production cars was the opposite way around to that of the prototype's single front wheel.

### Peel Trident (UK) 1964

DKW 49cc 2-stroke 4.2bhp engine
3-speed gearbox and 2 seats
Maximum speed: 30mph/48kph
Weight: 198lb/90kg
The dome was hinged at the front, and behind the seat was a luggage storage area, within the dome. The steering wheel had a single spoke. There were single and twin seat versions, and a few examples were produced with a larger, 125cc engine. With no provision for ventilation the dome misted up when occupied. In recent years, one of these cute little cars fetched over £30,000 at auction in London.

### Raleigh Safety Seven (UK) 1935

Raleigh 742cc 4-stroke 7.5bhp engine
3-speed gearbox and 2 seats
Maximum speed: 52mph/84kph
Weight: unknown
Raleigh was the origin of the company that eventually produced the Reliant range of three-wheelers. Raleigh, better remembered today for production of pedal cycles, made some small cars back in the 1930s when three wheels were thought to be a good way to achieve economy motoring. With a large diameter front wheel, the Safety Seven's turning circle was large. Prewar, Raleigh had also made some motorcycles. The next motorised Raleigh was the Roma scooter, which appeared in 1960, and was assembled under licence from Bianchi of Italy.

### Raleigh Van (UK) 1935

Raleigh 742cc 4-stroke 7.5bhp engine
3-speed gearbox and 2 seats
Maximum speed: 52mph/84kph
Weight: unknown
This van was a common sight on the UK's roads right into the 1950s, having been in production for many years. It continued to sell because its basic design was cheap to produce. The V twin engine drove the back axle via a shaft, and differential gearbox. It continued to give reliable service as the cheapest form of covered transport available at the time.

## Reliant Ant (UK) 1978

Reliant 848cc 4-stroke 40bhp engine
4-speed gearbox and 2 seats
Maximum speed: 65mph/105kph
Weight: dependent on selected load section
This was a light commercial development of the Reliant Robin chassis and engine, which could be fitted with various rear units such as flatbeds, pick-ups, refuse bins, road sweepers and tower wagons. There were even fire engine support vehicles. In 1977, commercial development was sold to a company called BTB, which did achieve many local authority and some export sales.

## Reliant Kitten (UK) 1978

Reliant 848cc 4-stroke 40bhp engine
4-speed gearbox and 4 seats
Maximum speed: 75mph/120kph
Weight: unknown
The Kitten was a four-wheeled version of the Reliant Robin three-wheeler for those with a full car licence. In every other respect it was identical to the Robin. As it cost more than the Robin – and other conventional small cars – to buy, it did not sell in large numbers. It was available as a saloon, estate or van.

## Reliant Kitten Van (UK) 1975

Reliant 848cc 4-stroke 40bhp engine
4-speed gearbox and 2 seats
Maximum speed: 75mph/120kph
Weight: unknown
The four-wheeled version of the Reliant Robin in van form; the last was made in 1981. Reliant owners seemed to stick with the marque once they had purchased one, so it was a sad day when all Reliant production finally ended in 2000. There have been several attempts to restart production as other concerns have taken over rights to the name. Today, Reliant imports microcars and small fun cars.

### Reliant Rebel (UK) 1967

Reliant 598cc 4-stroke 28bhp engine
4-speed gearbox and 2 seats
Maximum speed: 65mph/105kph
Weight: unknown

This was a plastic-bodied, four-wheeled car based on the then-current Reliant Regal three-wheeler model. It had an opening rear hatch with good load capability. Again, it cost much more than other mainstream cars so did not sell in large numbers. The 598cc engine was a rather slow performer. In 1975, the 848cc Reliant Kitten replaced the Rebel.

### Reliant Regal Mark 2 Coupé (UK) 1952

Reliant 747cc 4-stroke 16bhp engine
4-speed gearbox and 4 seats
Maximum speed: 60mph/97kph
Weight: 890lb/404kg

The bodywork was made of fibreglass mounted on a wooden frame, and styling became more modern with attractive, smooth, rounded lines. Available as a saloon and a coupé with an optional hard-top, there was more available space inside. Flashing direction indicators became standard. Confusingly, Reliant used the Regal name on various different types of vehicle. Motoring regulations in the UK and some other countries allowed vehicles under 900lb to be driven with a motorcycle licence, a crucial factor in Reliant's continued survival.

### Reliant Regal 325 (UK) 1962

Reliant 598cc 4-stroke 25bhp engine
4-speed gearbox and 4 seats
Maximum speed: 65mph/105kph
Weight: 896lb/406kg

The 325 nomenclature stood for three wheels and 25bhp. The rear of the car was styled like the then-current Ford Anglia and Bond Minicar whereby the base of the window lent inward, supposedly to keep it clearer in bad weather. The engine was advanced in being cast in aluminium by Reliant and not purchased from Austin, which had discontinued the original Seven engine used in previous Reliants. It was comparatively light and fuel-efficient. The 325 was also available as an estate and a van.

## Reliant Regal 325 Supervan (UK) 1973

Reliant 700cc 4-stroke 27bhp engine
4-speed gearbox and 4 seats
Maximum speed: 65mph/105kph
Weight: 890lb/404kg
Later models of the 325 had a 750cc version of the engine, increasing power to 31bhp. It became possible to monitor engine oil level at the dash panel; quite a useful and novel feature. Special editions of the van were produced: one sporty-looking version with stylish wheel discs and side trims was known as the Safari. Although it is hard to source exact details of the weight of several Reliant models, like all other similar vehicles they had to be below the 6cwt limit to qualify for cheaper road tax.

## Reliant Rialto (UK) 1984

Reliant 848cc 4-stroke 40bhp engine
4-speed gearbox and 4 seats
Maximum speed: 75mph/120kph
Weight: 892lb/405kg
The Rialto was really an upgraded Robin, also available as an estate and the last of the Reliant three-wheeler cars. The standard of interior trim was much higher than on previous Reliants. Confusion again resulted when certain versions of the Rialto were called Robins! Production reached a peak annual output of around 12,000 cars, which was good for a small company. Reliant had identified and exploited a gap in the market and, as a result was the UK's most successsful three-wheeler manufacturer, eventually closing in 2000 after 50 years of production.

## Reliant Robin (UK) 1980

Reliant 848cc 4-stroke 40bhp engine
4-speed gearbox and 4 seats
Maximum speed: 75mph/120kph
Weight: 890lb/404kg
The car that Reliant is best remembered for and the one most comedians joke about! It was nevertheless an economical and very practical vehicle which offerd near-standard internal space and facilities, with much improved road manners, compared with earlier Reliants. The design came from Ogle, also the designer of the Bond Bug which used the same chassis. There were van and estate variants.

## Reliant Robin Estate (UK) 1980

Reliant 848cc 4-stroke 40bhp engine
4-speed gearbox and 4 seats
Maximum speed: 75mph/120kph
Weight: 893lb/405kg
Affectionately known as the Plastic Pig, the Robin was
a very practical car in estate form, and found a market
in Europe where motoring regulations similar to
those of the UK gave it advantages. Reliant also had
a market in larger-engined sports cars, but a modern
replacement for the successful Scimitar did not fulfil
expectations, resulting in serious survival problems in
1990.

## Rollera (France) 1958

Comprena 98cc 2-stroke 5bhp engine
3-speed gearbox and 1 seat
Maximum speed: 50mph/80kph
Weight: 187lb/85kg
This interesting vehicle came from Egon Brutsch,
German designer of the Mopeta and Spatz. Only
eight were produced in Germany and only three are
known of today. The French company STE also made
a handful, and shown is the only known survivor of
these. It is strange that at the time the Rollera was
produced, it found few buyers. Today, collectors rush
to spend vast sums of money to acquire one; recently,
an example sold at auction for £23,000. Clive
Sinclair's 1990 C5 was hoping for the same market ...

## Rovin D4 (France) 1951

Rovin 462cc 4-stroke 13bhp engine
3-speed gearbox and 2 seats
Maximum speed: 50mph/80kph
Weight: 866lb/394kg
Rovin had made a reputation for himself as an
inspired microcar designer and producer since 1946.
Back in the 1920s, he had been associated with
several cyclecars, the economy vehicles of that time.
The D4's engine was a water-cooled flat twin; the car
had cable-operated brakes; the body was made of
steel; the wheels were cast aluminium. This little car
was made until 1959.

## Scootacar Mark 1 (UK) 1960

Villiers 197cc 2-stroke 8.6bhp engine
4-speed gearbox and 2 seats
Maximum speed: 50mph/80kph
Weight: 504lb/228kg
The Scootacar was made by the Hunslet Locomotive company in Leeds. It had a fibreglass body with a single door. The driver sat above the central engine on a padded cover with a passenger behind. There was space for two small children at the rear. A spare wheel could be mounted externally below the rear window. The car had handlebar steering. The designer had previously been involved with an earlier unsuccessful but interesting microcar called the Rodley.

## Scootacar Mark 2 (UK) 1961

Villiers 197cc 2-stroke 8.6bhp engine
4-speed gearbox and 2 seats
Maximum speed: 50mph/80kph
Weight: 502lb/228kg
The Mark 2 had more interior room than the Mark 1. The body was larger and more rounded in shape. The driver now had a separate moulded seat, and the rear bench seat was larger and more comfortable. There was also a very desirable 16bhp, 324cc, Mark 3 version, capable of speeds of 68mph (109kph). This design deserved to be more successful than it was, and is remembered with affection. The last Scootacar was produced in 1965.

## Seat 600 (Spain) 1971

Seat 767cc 4-stroke 32bhp engine
4-speed gearbox and 4 seats
Maximum speed: 68mph/110kph
Weight: 1276lb/580kg
The Italian Fiat company was very successful at licensing production of its car designs to other countries, and this was the Fiat 600D made in Spain from 1957 until 1973. The 600 had a rear mounted engine, and was easily recognised by its larger, more effective headlamps, which improved the car's appearance. Today, Seat is part of the Volkswagen group and no longer associated with Fiat.

## Simson Duo (East Germany) 1976

IWL 50cc 2-stroke engine
3-speed gearbox and 3 seats
Maximum speed: 31mph/50kph
Weight: unknown
Specially imported from its former home behind the
Iron Curtain to the UK by an enthusiast following
the fall of the Berlin wall. The fuel tank lives behind
the top right-hand legshield. There is room for two
rear passengers with legs extended beside the driver.
Recognisable East German Simson moped parts were
used.

## Smart Brabus (France) 2003

Mercedes 698cc 4-stroke 74bhp engine
6-speed gearbox and 2 seats
Maximum speed: 94mph/151kph
Weight: 1595lb/725kg
The Brabus version of the Smart is a higher
performance model based on the Passion which
benefits from extra body styling feature, larger
wheels and wider tyres. The front has a spoiler,
and various other body styling add-ons give it a
sportier appearance. In top-of-the-range form the
Brabus becomes a very expensive vehicle to buy,
but does offer excellent performance in tandem with
individuality and style.

## Smart Cabriolet (France) 2001

Mercedes 599cc 4-stroke 61bhp engine
6-speed gearbox and 2 seats
Maximum speed: 84mph/135kph
Weight: 1628lb/740kg
Based on the Passion, this model has a power-
operated fabric sunroof, revised front suspension,
headlamps, and style. It is especially attractive to
those who want economic open air motoring with
panache. Like all the Smart models, the flexible
plastic body panels can be changed for those of a
different colour within an hour.

## Smart Passion (France) 1999

Mercedes 599cc 4-stroke 61bhp engine
6-speed gearbox and 2 seats
Maximum speed: 84mph/135kph
Weight: 1595lb/725kg
The Deluxe version with more power and accessories, including automatic and manual sequential 6-speed gear selection, air conditioning, a glass roof with adjustable sunblind, traction control, alloy wheels and fog Lamps. It covers nearly 60 miles per gallon of petrol, has low emissions and tax, cheap insurance, non-rusting bodywork, and can park in the smallest of spaces.

## Smart Pulse Diesel (France) 2000

Mercedes 799cc diesel 46bhp engine
6-speed gearbox and 2 seats
Maximum speed: 84mph/135kph
Weight: 1606lb/730kg
The diesel version of the left-hand-drive Smart became available in the UK via various unofficial importers to meet customer demand. When, however, official importers were appointed in 2001 and right-hand-drive became available, it was decided not to import this model any longer (probably because the 57mpg achieved by the petrol version was thought to be more than sufficient). The Pulse model slotted between the basic Pure and the top-of-the-line Passion. Extras could be added, and, in fact, this particular car started out with black body panels, and now has alloy wheels.

## Smart Pure (France) 2000

Mercedes 599cc 4-stroke 50bhp engine
6-speed gearbox and 2 seats
Maximum speed: 84mph/135kph
Weight: 1573lb/715kg
Smart is a revolution in microcar design and has brought the concept right up-to-date. Its reward has been sales figures never before achieved by a microcar. The basic model shown is nevertheless highly specified with ABS and an immobiliser. The windows are electrically-operated. The manufacturer is called MCC, which stands for Micro Compact Car, and was originally associated with the Swiss watch company, Swatch, then Volkswagen. It is now part of the Daimler Chrysler group, which incorporates Mercedes, which designed and makes the engines.

## Smart Roadster (France) 2003

Mercedes 698cc 4-stroke 80bhp engine
6-speed gearbox and 2 seats
Maximum speed: 109mph/175kph
Weight: 1738lb/790kg

A new design of lightweight sports car that has been developed from the Smart car. The intention has been to recreate the fun of driving first associated with 1950s small sports cars such as the Berkeley, but with all modern driving conveniences. The classic mid-engine, rear-wheel-drive layout with low centre of gravity gives real driving pleasure at minimum expense. Detachable roof support bars locate in the front boot, when total open-top motoring is desired.

## Smart Roadster Coupé (France) 2003

Mercedes 698cc 4-stroke 80bhp engine
6-speed gearbox and 2 seats
Maximum speed: 112mph/180kph
Weight: 1782lb/810kg

Whereas the Roadster version comes complete with an electrically-operated fabric soft-top, which folds out of sight into the rear boot, the Roadster Coupé has a two-piece removable hard-top which can be stored, also in the rear boot. A rear hinged glass roof panel gives additional internal storage space. Both versions have a second front luggage storage area, and easily detachable plastic body panels.

## SMZ SZA Cabriolet (Russia) 1962

SMZ 346cc 2-stroke 7bhp engine
4-speed gearbox and 2 seats
Maximum speed: unknown
Weight: unknown

This little car was made in large numbers, and similar designs appear to have been made in other USSR countries such as Poland where it was known as the Smynk. Few, if any, escaped to the west. This example was photographed in Moscow when I saw it by the roadside there in 1964. It does have a rather cute and utilitarian appearance.

## Solyto TC7 (France) 1959

Ultima 125cc 2-stroke engine
4-speed gearbox and 1 seat
Maximum speed: 31mph/50kph
Weight: 330lb/150kg

With styling reminiscent of 1930s automobiles, this little van has a basic canvas driving seat, and the engine is sited above the front wheel. The fuel tank and its filler cap sit on the right-hand dashboard. It had a carrying capacity of 200kg (440lb). A licence was not required to drive it on French roads. It has been described as beautifully ugly!

## Subaru 360 (Japan) 1965

Subaru 360cc 4-stroke 25bhp engine
4-speed gearbox and 4 seats
Maximum speed: 50mph/80kph
Weight: 851lb/387kg

Japan has experienced many periods of microcar fascination, and has produced many interesting designs that were never seen in Europe, some by really large manufacturers. This particular car came into the UK from Singapore, where it was seen by an enthusiast. The 360 was available as a van, pick-up and convertible, and also as a higher spec sports model.

## Suzuki SC100 (Japan) 1980

Suzuki 547cc 4-stroke 31bhp engine
4-speed gearbox and 4 seats
Maximum speed: 65mph/105kph
Weight: unknown

Cute modern and economic, the SC100 sold well in the UK, and today has a strong owners and supporters club. It was one of the first little Japanese cars to catch public attention in the UK. In 1981, Suzuki also made the interesting CV1 microcar, a very traditional-looking bubblecar; sadly, unavailable in the UK.

## Trabant 600 Kombi (East Germany) 1963

Trabant 594cc 2-stroke 22bhp engine
3-speed gearbox and 4 seats
Maximum speed: 62mph/99kph
Weight: unknown

The larger capacity engine fitted in the Trabant P50 was accompanied by a change of title to 600. This was the estate version which was quite a practical vehicle with a low, flat loading area. The dark green colour was very characteristic of Trabants of the period.

## Trabant 601 Kombi (East Germany) 1962

Trabant 594cc 2-stroke 22bhp engine
3-speed gearbox and 4 seats
Maximum speed: 62mph/99kph
Weight: unknown

The estate version of the famous 'Trabby' which kept the two-stroke car alive in East Germany long after the DKW and Wartburg had died out but, with the fall of the Berlin Wall, this, too, died in 1990. This model was very characteristic of an economic little car designed to be affordable by everyone. Its popping, two-stroke exhaust made it sound like so many of the late 1950s and early '60s UK microcars.

## Trabant 601 (East Germany) 1980

Trabant 594cc 2-stroke 22bhp engine
3-speed gearbox and 4 seats
Maximum speed: 62mph/99kph
Weight: unknown

The 601 body was made from a plastic and paper material called Duraplas, and fitted onto a steel chassis. The waiting list for one of these was several years long, due to the fact that it was practically the only car available to the common man. This vanished when western cars became available, following collapse of the East/West divide.

## Trabant Kübelwagon (East Germany) 1990

Trabant 594cc 2-stroke 22bhp engine
3-speed gearbox and 4 seats
Maximum speed: 62mph/99kph
Weight: unknown

This model was famous for its use by East German border guards, who had the authority to shoot anyone trying to leave the country. It did have fuel injection which must be unique on a two-stroke! Modern European air pollution restrictions now do not permit new two-stroke-engined cars to exist in any form. The Trabant has a loyal following and many have been imported into the UK by enthusiasts since collapse of the Berlin Wall.

## Trabant P50 (East Germany) 1959

Trabant 594cc 2-stroke 22bhp engine
3-speed gearbox and 4 seats
Maximum speed: 62mph/99kph
Weight: unknown

Trabants were produced by an offshoot of the prewar DKW company which split after the division of Germany into East and West. DKW had years of experience with large, two-stroke engines in cars and continued to develop them while they gradually died out in the West. It took the fall of the Berlin Wall thirty years later to finally kill off those oil-burning engines in cars. The last Trabants were fitted with West German, VW four-stroke engines.

## Tritech Schmitt (UK) 1997

Honda 244cc 4-stroke 17bhp engine
Auto gearbox and 2 seats
Maximum speed: 65mph/105kph
Weight: 594lb/270kg

This is a modern kit car that very closely resembles the famous Messerschmitt bubble car of the 1960s. It has a larger, more powerful engine than the original with an automatic gearbox. The hydraulically-operated brakes are larger, too. In many ways the Schmitt is an updated design of an original classic, providing the nostalgia of the Messerschmitt yet better suited for use on today's roads.

## Tritech Zetta (UK) 1997

Honda 244cc 4-stroke 17bhp engine
Auto gearbox and 2 seats
Maximum speed: 63mph/101kph
Weight: 660lb/300kg

The Zetta is a modern replica of the BMW Isetta, fitted with a water-cooled engine, automatic gearbox and better brakes. The engine, unlike the original, sits along the centre of the chassis for better roadholding. The bodywork is made from fibreglass. A larger capacity Kawasaki engine with manual gearbox is also available.

## Trojan (UK) 1962

Heinkel 198cc 4-stroke 10bhp engine
4speed gearbox and 4 seats
Maximum speed: 50mph/80kph
Weight: 583lb/265kg

This is the Heinkel bubblecar made in England from 1961 to 1965. The original German production was transferred to Ireland in 1958, following legal problems with Heinkel's arch rival, Isetta. When production ceased in Ireland, it restarted in England, which showed confidence in the future market for microcars when many other makes were experiencing a decline in sales. Trojan produced both left- and right-hand-drive versions, and some were exported to other countries, including Germany.

## Trojan Convertible (UK) 1962

Heinkel 204cc 2-stroke 10.5bhp engine
4-speed gearbox and 4 seats
Maximum speed: 50mph/80kph
Weight: 572lb/260kg

The bubbleless bubblecar! In fine weather it was great, and a lot quieter to drive as engine noise was swept away by the slipstream. In the saloon version, the engine top cover was inside the dome with the driver. The folding fabric roof had flexible side and rear windows. Unlike the Isetta, the steering column was not fixed to the door.

## Trojan Van (UK) 1964

Heinkel 198cc 4-stroke 10bhp engine
4-speed gearbox and 4 seats
Maximum speed: 50mph/80kph
Weight: 589lb/268kg
The large, opening rear door afforded access to the empty floor behind the front seats. The bubble was now made of fibreglass with a window on each side. Toward the end of production, engine selection depended on availability from the German Heinkel factory, but all were similarly powered. Trojan production ceased in 1965. In total, not as many Heinkel bubblecars were produced as Isettas, although many tens of thousands of each were made in several different countries.

## Velam (France) 1957

ISO 236cc 2-stroke 10.5bhp engine
4-speed gearbox and 2 seats
Maximum speed: 53mph/85kph
Weight: 756lb/343kg
The French version of the Isetta, affectionately known as the Tortoise. The Velam name meant "Vehicle with a light motor". The original Iso Isetta design concept was used but in a re-designed body. It had two closely-coupled, eleven inch wheels at the rear. The speedometer was located in the centre of the rotating steering wheel. When pressed, a push-button located ahead of the right-hand headlamp opened the door. A convertible model was available with a fabric roof, as was a deluxe version known as the Ecrin. Production came to an end in 1959.

## Velorex (Czechoslovakia) 1968

Jawa 344cc 2-stroke 16bhp engine
4-speed gearbox and 2 seats
Maximum speed: 50mph/80kph
Weight: 506lb/230kg
This little car was first seen in 1954, and continued in production until 1971, during which time it must have sold many more examples than some conventional cars. Initially, it had a 125cc, then a 250cc, Jawa two-stroke engine. The engine was at the rear where it was very accessible. The whole body was canvas stretched over a steel tube frame. I love a sentence from the English version of the original manual which says that the car is designed "For two pieces of man and two brave children". There was also a much dearer but less popular version of the car which was made with the same mechanics but covered in a heavier, conventional steel body.

## Vespa 400 (France) 1959

Piaggio 393cc 2-stroke 20bhp engine
4-speed gearbox and 4 seats
Maximum speed: 50mph/80kph
Weight: 792lb/360kg

This car was made by ACMA which also produced Vespa scooters under licence in France. It was designed by Piaggio in Italy but produced in France only to avoid upsetting Fiat at home. It gave the microcar concept a boost in generally providing more power without loss in economy. It had a roll-back fabric roof. The battery was located in a pull-out tray from the front grille. Production ended in 1961 after around 30,000 examples had been made.

## Victoria 250 (West Germany) 1957

Victoria 245cc 2-stroke 14bhp engine
5-speed gearbox and 2 seats
Maximum speed: 59mph/97kph
Weight: 935lb/425kg

This was an improved Spatz with an electrically-operated gearbox, and was very advanced for its time. Production costs did not allow the car to be sold cheaply, which obviously made a difference to the number sold. Toward the end of production, another firm became involved with the finance and the car's name changed briefly to Burgfalke. Production ceased in 1957. Today, thanks to its stylish and undated appearance, the Victgoria 250 is one of the most sought-after microcars.

## Webster Bug (UK) 1993

Reliant 848cc 4-stroke 40bhp engine
4-speed gearbox and 2 seats
Maximum speed: 75mph/120kph
Weight: unknown

This was the standard Webster Bug which, unlike the original, was made with four wheels and solid, lockable side doors. The front wheels and suspension came from those fitted on the Mini. Adding a fourth wheel was intended to provide the Bond Bug with greater stability, security and control. Sales, however, did not turn out to be as keen as was hoped.

## Webster Bug Sports (UK) 1992

Reliant 848cc 4-stroke 40bhp engine
4-speed gearbox and 2 seats
Maximum speed: 75mph/120kph
Weight: unknown

Mike Webster, who had a great classic scooter collection, also had an interest in microcars. In the 1970s, the Bond Bug was one of the microcar makes that disappeared. In the 1990s, Mike thought that there was enough interest and life left in the design to make it viable for him to become financially involved in recreating the car as a four-wheeler. Shown here is his completely open sporting variant, with tiny twin flyscreens and a waterproof interior. The green prototype was affectionately known as Kermit!

## Willam Farmer (France) 1971

Innocenti 123cc 2-stroke 5.6bhp engine
4-speed gearbox and 2 seats
Maximum speed: 43mph/70kph
Weight: 728lb/331kg

The designer of this model – the president of the French Lambretta company (name unknown) – was one of the foremost microcar advocates in France. He decided in 1967 to use Lambretta parts in making a useful economic small car, a saloon model called the City. Production actually occurred in Italy, and the body was made of fibreglass on a steel frame. In 1968, he introduced a convertible version, calling it the Farmer, and went on to design further microcars, including one with the strange title of Baldi Frog, which could have a 125cc, 302cc or 595cc engine. A Mark 2 Farmer was produced in 1975. Other Willam microcars were produced, and marketed and sold in other countries right up until the 1980s.

## Williams TC1 (UK) 1995

BMC 998cc 2-stroke 55bhp engine
4-speed gearbox and 2 seats
Maximum speed: 75mph/120kph
Weight: unknown

A one-off car designed and built by Hugh Williams of south Wales at a time when there weren't any high powered microcars on the market. The TC1 uses the engine and other parts from a Mini. There was some commercial interest in the car but, sadly, production did not follow; definitely a missed marketing opportunity as this was an attractive and interesting vehicle.

## Zundapp Janus (West Germany) 1958

Zundapp 248cc 2-stroke 14bhp engine
4-speed gearbox and 4 seats
Maximum speed: 50mph/80kph
Weight: 935lb/425kg

Named after the Roman god Janus who had one countenance facing forward and one backward, just as this car has a door at each end. The engine fits in-between the two seat backrests. This layout was first devised by the Dornier company in Germany for its Delta microcar; in this way four people can be carried, all with easy access. The car was made in 1957 and 1958 only when the factory closed, after nearly 7000 had been produced. They were briefly advertised in the UK though it is doubtful that any were actually imported.

# Scooter & microcar timelines

Sometimes a scooter was better known by the manufacturer's name, such as Heinkel and James, and sometimes by the model name, such as Capri and Diana. I have endeavoured to list scooters by the name which is best known. When a manufacturer changed the name but used a similar bodyshell – such as DKR with the Dove, Pegasus, Defiant and Manx – I have listed the original name only.

I have tried to give an idea of the rise and fall in popularity of each model as the years passed. so if a particular scooter name disappears from the listing it's because it has been discontinued, or, in some cases, was not imported for that particular year, such as the Iso and Bella. Some models were only briefly imported in small numbers to test the water (Roletta and Goggo), and some were available at select dealers rather than nationwide. Still others – such as the BSA Beeza and Harper – were advertised as widely available yet did not appear at all in showrooms due to production problems, or a change in company policy.

Vespa and Lambretta produced a large range of models over many years, so I have simply used these names in the main list, separately listing all of the models and available dates later.

A Vespa Rally 180 and Lambretta TV 175 seem to have fallen out ...

| 1952 | 1953 | 1954 | 1955 | 1956 |
|------|------|------|------|------|
| Corgi | Bella | Ariete | Beeza | Adler |
| Lambretta | Corgi | Bella | Bella | Bambi |
| Scoiattolo | Lambretta | Corgi | Britax | Bella |
| Vespa | Oscar | Goggo | Corgi | Contessa |
| | Vespa | Harper | Dayton | Dandy |
| | | Lambretta | Lambretta | Dayton |
| | | Vespa | Parilla | Diana |
| | | | Paris Nice | Heinkel |
| | | | Roletta | Hermes |
| | | | Vespa | Hobby |
| | | | | Keift |
| | | | | Kreidler |
| | | | | Lambretta |
| | | | | Moby |
| | | | | Nicky |
| | | | | Parilla |
| | | | | Piatti |
| | | | | Prima |
| | | | | Progress |
| | | | | Puch |
| | | | | Rumi |
| | | | | Vespa |

Opposite table: Mopeds experienced a similar surge in popularity. Some of the smaller engined, so-called scooters, such as the Britax Scooterette and the Kreidler R50, were really glorified mopeds so have not been included here.

| 1957 | 1958 | 1959 | 1960 |
|---|---|---|---|
| Adler | Adler | Bambi | Bambi |
| Bambi | Alpino | Bella | Bella |
| Bella | Bambi | Bond | Bond |
| Binz | Bella | BSA Sunbeam | BSA Sunbeam |
| Contessa | Bitri | Dandy | Capri |
| Dandy | Chicco | Dayton | Dandy |
| Dayton | Contessa | Dayton Flamenco | Dayton |
| Diana | Dandy | Diana | Dayton Flamenco |
| Dunkley | Dayton | DKR Dove | Diana |
| Heinkel | Diana | Dunkley | DKR Dove |
| Hobby | DKR Dove | Excelsior 1 | Dunkley |
| Keift | Dunkley | Guizzo | Excelsior 2 |
| Lambretta | Guzzi | Heinkel | Heinkel |
| Maicoletta | Heinkel | Iso | Iso |
| Maicomobile | Hobby | Jawa Cezeta | James |
| Moby | Iso | Lambretta | Jawa Cezeta |
| Nicky | Lambretta | Maicoletta | Lambretta |
| Parilla | Maicoletta | Manurhin | Maicoletta |
| Peugeot | Maicomobile | Moby | Manurhin |
| Piatti | Maserati | Panther | Moby |
| Pippin | Moby | Peugeot | Panther |
| Prima D | Parilla | Phoenix | Peugeot |
| Progress | Peugeot | Prima D | Phoenix |
| Puch Rl | Phoenix | Prima 3kl | Prima D |
| Rumi | Piatti | Prior | Prima 3kl |
| Terrot | Pippin | Puch Alpine | Prior |
| Vespa | Prima D | Rumi | Puch Alpine |
| Wabo | Prior | Sun Geni | Puch Cheetah |
| | Progress | Sun Wasp | Rumi |
| | Prima 3kl | Terrot | Sun Gen |
| | Puch Rl | Triumph Tigress | Sun Wasp |
| | Rumi | Vespa | Triumph Tigress |
| | Sun Geni | | Vespa |
| | Terrot | | |
| | TWN Tessy | | |
| | Vespa | | |

| 1961 | 1962 | 1963 | 1964 |
|------|------|------|------|
| Ambassador | Ambassador | Aermacchi | Aermacchi |
| Bambi | Bambi | Bella | Bella |
| Bella | BSA Sunbeam | BSA Sunbeam | BSA Sunbeam |
| Bond | Capri | Capri | Capri |
| BSA Sunbeam | Conny | Diana | DKR Capella |
| Capri | Dandy | DKR Capella | Guizzo |
| Conny | Diana | Garelli | Heinkel |
| Dandy | DKR Capella | Guizzo | Heinkel A2 |
| Diana | Excelsior 2 | Heinkel | Heinkel 150 |
| DKR Capella | Heinkel | Heinkel A2 | Iso |
| Excelsior 2 | Heinkel A2 | Heinkel 150 | James |
| Heinkel | Heinkel 150 | Iso | Jawa Manet |
| Iso | James | James | Lambretta |
| James | Jawa Manet | Jawa Manet | Laverda |
| Jawa Cezeta | KTM Pony | KTM Pony | Maicoletta |
| Jawa Manet | Lambretta | Lambretta | Motobi |
| Lambretta | Laverda | Laverda | Paloma |
| Laverda | Maicoletta | Maicoletta | Panther |
| Maicoletta | Moby | Motobi | Phoenix |
| Manurhin | Panther | NSU Prima 3KL | Puch Alpine |
| Moby | Phoenix | Paloma | Puch Cheetah |
| Panther | Prima D | Panther | Raleigh Roma |
| Phoenix | Prima 3KL | Phoenix | Triumph Tigress |
| Prima D | Puch Alpine | Puch Cheetah | Triumph Tina |
| Prima 3KL | Puch Cheetah | Raleigh Roma | Velocette |
| Prior | Raleigh Roma | Rumi | Vespa |
| Puch Alpine | Rumi | Triumph Tina | |
| Puch Cheetah | Triumph Tigress | Triumph Tigress | |
| Raleigh Roma | Trobike | Velocette | |
| Rumi | Velocette | Vespa | |
| Sun Wasp | Vespa | | |
| Triumph Tigress | | | |
| Trobike | | | |
| Velocette | | | |
| Vespa | | | |

| 1965 | 1966 | 1967 | 1968 | 1969 |
|---|---|---|---|---|
| Capri | Capri | Capri | Heinkel A2 | Lambretta |
| Heinkel | Heinkel A2 | Heinkel A2 | Lambretta | Vespa |
| Heinkel A2 | Heinkel 150 | Heinkel 150 | Puch Cheetah | |
| Heinkel 150 | Jawa Manet | Jawa Manet | Vespa | |
| Iso | Lambretta | Lambretta | | |
| Jawa Manet | Laverda | Maicoletta | | |
| Lambretta | Maicoletta | Motobi | | |
| Laverda | Motobi | Puch Cheetah | | |
| Maicoletta | Puch Alpine | Puch Pony | | |
| Motobi | Puch Cheetah | Triumph T10 | | |
| Puch Alpine | Puch Pony | Vespa | | |
| Puch Cheetah | Triumph T10 | | | |
| Puch Pony | Vespa | | | |
| Triumph T10 | | | | |
| Vespa | | | | |

## Date listings for Vespa and Lambretta

Vespa and Lambretta, the two most popular makes, between them produced a large range of models over the many years covered in this book. The following is a dating list for these two makes.

| Vespa (Piaggio) | Lambretta (Innocenti) |
|---|---|
| 1950  Rod | 1951  125 LC 125 LD s1 |
| 1954  G GL2 | 1953  125 LD s2 |
| 1955  GS 150 VS1 | 1954  125 D 150 D 125 LDA 150 LD s2 |
| 1956  42 L2 GS 150 VS2 | 1955  150 LDA |
| 1957  92 L2 GS 150 VS3 GS 150 VD2 TS | 1957  125 LD s3 150 LD s3 |
| 1958  GS 150 VS4 Clubman | 1958  Li 125 Li 150 TV 175 |
| 1959  152L2 43 GS 150 VS5 NEW 150 | 1959  Li 125 s2 Li 150 s2 LD s4 |
| 1962  GS 160 MK1 Sportique | 1960  TV 175 s2 |
| 1963  GS 160 MK2 232L2 | 1961  Rallymaster |
| 1964  90 STD | 1962  Li 125 s3 Li 150 s3 TV 175 s3 |
| 1965  GL 150 SS180 Sprint 150 | 1963  TV 200 Li 150 sp Pacemaker |
| 1966  90 SS 125 VMA | 1964  Cento J50 J125 |
| 1969  Super 150 | 1965  SX 125 |
| 1970  180 Rally Primavera | 1966  SX 150 SX 200 J125 Starstream |
| 1972  90 Racer 125 Super | 1968  J50DL Vega Cometa |
| 1973  200 Rally | 1969  GP 125 GP 150 GP 200 |
| | 1970  J50 SP |

Vespa continued with production and is still a major scooter manufacturer today, its products available and popular for the last fifty years. Sadly, Lambretta was forced to cease scooter production in 1972 due to many labour disputes and management sell-outs. The factory turned to car production and the scooter production machinery was purchased by an Indian company. Thereafter, from time-to-time, batches of Indian-made Lambrettas were imported to the UK to meet the demand that still existed. Lambrettas were also manufactured in Spain until well into the 1980s and imported to the UK, where a thriving restoration market for Lambrettas sprang up to keep these fine machines on the road. Vespa and Lambretta models were regularly seen on the UK roads and were soon the only makes that were.

## Microcar date listings

The vehicles included here – as in the rest of the book – are those whose owners feel an affinity with microcars and regularly attend microcar rallies, even though, strictly speaking, their vehicles, such as some Reliants and the baby Fiats, may not be true microcars.

Unlike scooters, microcar availability was generally not nationwide, and some models were never seen at all in certain parts of the UK.

| 1952 | 1953 | 1954 | 1955 | 1956 |
|---|---|---|---|---|
| AC Petite | AC Petite | AC Petite | AC Petite | AC Petite |
| Bond | Allard | Allard | Allard | Astra |
| Fiat 500 | Bond | Bond | Bond | Berkeley |
| Reliant | Fiat 500 | Fairthorpe | Fairthorpe | Bond |
| | Messerschmitt | Fiat 500 | Fiat Multipla | Fairthorpe |
| | Pashley | Goggomobile | Fiat 500 | Fiat Multipla |
| | Reliant | Gordon | Fuldamobile | Fiat 500 |
| | | Messerschmitt | Goggomobile | Goggomobile |
| | | Pashley | Gordon | Gordon |
| | | Reliant | Isetta | Heinkel |
| | | Rodley | Messerschmitt | Isetta |
| | | | Pashley | Messerschmitt |
| | | | Peel | Opperman |
| | | | Powerdrive | Pashley |
| | | | Reliant | Peel |
| | | | Rodley | Powerdrive |
| | | | | Reliant |
| | | | | Rodley |
| | | | | Tourette |

It is interesting to note how the rise and fall in the fortunes of true microcars so closely followed that of scooters. Interest in and demand for microcars – as affordable, convenient, covered transport – began to increase in the early 1950s and reached a peak about ten years later. Around five years further on the decline began and the fall was quicker than the rise, due mainly to the fact that incomes in general were higher and prices of second-hand conventional cars were lower. Unfortunately, the trade-in price of a microcar was next to nothing.

In the forefront of popularity in the UK was the Bond Minicar which remained in production to the end. It was the first and last of the classic microcars, the most successful and, in many ways, the best. Laurie Bond designed several other microcars during the same period, such as the Berkeley and the Unicar, and must be considered the hero of the time. He also designed the Sherpa scooter.

Other stars arrived: the German bubblecars, Isetta, Heinkel and Messerschmitt. In spite of widespread popularity and success, however, they did not survive for as long.

Other British successes were the Scootacar Berkeley and Frisky, and it was difficult to understand at the time quite why and how the market for them just disappeared.

On paper it would appear that the Goggomobile was the best UK seller as it was in Germany, but as it was not a three-wheeler, full road tax was payable and a full driving licence needed, which greatly restricted sales. In fact, apart from a few years, it was not widely available at all except on special order at some dealers. The manufacturers of other makes which began life as four-wheelers, such as the Isetta and Frisky, were quick to produce three-wheeled versions to appeal to a much wider market.

In the UK there wasn't a microcar survivor as there was with the scooter and Vespa, and it was thirty years before a resurgence in the UK market for this individual form of economic transport.

In the larger machines, Reliant, of course, did survive right up to the end of the century but although it was an economic three-wheeler, it was also a rather different class of vehicle to the true, small, tiny-engined and air-cooled microcars.

A very rare microcar in the UK. This little Daihatsu is a personal import.

| 1957 | 1958 | 1959 | 1960 |
|------|------|------|------|
| AC Petite | AC Petite | Astra | Astra |
| Astra | Astra | Berkeley | Berkeley |
| Berkeley | Berkeley | Bianchi | Bianchi |
| Bianchi | Bianchi | BMW 600 | BMW 700 |
| BMW 600 | BMW 600 | Bond | Bond |
| Bond | Bond | Coronet | Coronet |
| Bruetsch | Coronet | Fairthorpe | Fairthorpe |
| Coronet | Fairthorpe | Fiat Multipla | Fiat Multipla |
| Fairthorpe | Fiat Multipla | Fiat 500 | Fiat 500 |
| Fiat Multipla | Fiat 500 | Frisky | Frisky |
| Fiat 500 | Frisky | Goggomobile | Goggomobile |
| Frisky | Goggomobile | Heinkel | Heinkel |
| Goggomobile | Gordon | Isetta | Isetta |
| Gordon | Heinkel | Lloyd Alex | Lloyd Alex |
| Heinkel | Isetta | Messerschmitt | Messerschmitt |
| Isetta | Lloyd Alex | Nobel | Nobel |
| Messerschmitt | Messerschmitt | NSU Prinz | NSU Prinz |
| Opperman | NSU Prinz | NSU SP Prinz | NSU SP Prinz |
| Peel | Opperman | Opperman | Peel |
| Powerdrive | Peel | Peel | Reliant |
| Reliant | Powerdrive | Reliant | Scootacar |
| Seat 600 | Reliant | Scootacar | Seat 600 |
| Tourette | Scootacar | Seat 600 | |
| | Seat 600 | | |

1965 was the last year it was possible to easily buy a microcar, by the end of the 1960s true microcars simply did not feature in dealer showrooms. Some enthusiasts managed to keep running a small selection of models, whilst others stockpiled them; it was obvious, to all, though, that the modern motorist wanted more comfort and performance from his transport. Bond, Messerschmitt, and Heinkel Trojan owners clubs soldiered on, still holding their own annual rallies.

During the 1970s microcars occasionally appeared at general classic vehicle rallies, becoming a more frequent occurrence as restorations increased and interest was revived.

| 1961 | 1962 | 1963 | 1964 |
|------|------|------|------|
| Bianchi | Bianchi | Bianchi | Bianchi |
| BMW 700 | BMW 700 | BMW 700 | BMW 700 |
| Bond | Bond | Bond | Bond |
| Fiat 500 | Fiat 500 | Fiat 500 | Fiat 500 |
| Frisky | Frisky | Frisky | Frisky |
| Goggomobile | Goggomobile | Goggomobile | Goggomobile |
| Isetta | Isetta | Messerschmitt | Messerschmitt |
| Lloyd Alex | Lloyd Alex | NSU SP Prinz | NSU SP Prinz |
| Messerschmitt | Messerschmitt | Peel | Peel |
| Nobel | Nobel | Reliant | Reliant |
| NSU SP Prinz | NSU SP Prinz | Scootacar | Scootacar |
| Peel | Peel | Seat 600 | Trojan |
| Reliant | Reliant | Trojan | |
| Scootacar | Scootacar | | |
| Seat 600 | Seat 600 | | |
| Trojan | Trojan | | |

| 1965 | 1966 | 1967 | 1968 | 1969 |
|------|------|------|------|------|
| Bianchi | Bianchi | Bianchi | Bianchi | Bianchi |
| BMW 700 | Bond | Bond 875 | Bond 875 | Bond 875 |
| Bond | Bond 875 | Fiat 500 | Fiat 500 | Fiat 500 |
| Bond 875 | Fiat 500 | Goggomobile | Goggomobile | Goggomobile |
| Fiat 500 | Goggomobile | NSU SP Prinz | Honda 600 | Honda 600 |
| Goggomobile | NSU SP Prinz | Reliant | Reliant | Reliant |
| NSU SP Prinz | Peel | Suzuki 100 | Suzuki 100 | Suzuki 100 |
| Peel | Reliant | | | Tici |
| Reliant | | | | |
| Scootacar | | | | |
| Trojan | | | | |

# Picture gallery

An IWL Pitty scooter is dwarfed by a period BSA a
Cefartha Castle in south Wales

An Aixam microcar and 1960s Bristol Britannia airliner at Kemble airfield in Gloucestershire.

A pretty little Bianchi Bianchino at a microcar rally in Bath.

A young enthusiast
admires the Berkeley T60
microcar – and with good reason.

In early March an Isetta is
pictured in a winter wonderland
scene at a Weston Park rally.

Atten-shun, you 'orrible little car! A Trojan bubblecar in military get-up at a microcar rally in Bath.

A Scootacar MK3 receives some spit and polish at a microcar rally at Bath.

A Messerschmitt Tiger and period transporter, a Citroën H long wheelbase van, at a rally in Oxfordshire.

An open Bond minicar MK F and Messerschmitt KR200 at Crich in Derbyshire.

A Trojan Cabin Cruiser and a Messerschmitt KR200 make a
lovely picture at Castle Combe in Wiltshire.

A smart Passion rests on the quay at Mevagissey in Cornwall.

Two fine examples of the BMW 600 at a microcar rally at Weston Park in Shropshire.

A Bond minicar MK A at Kemble in Gloucestershire.

A cheeky little Mopetta and rather more austere Larmar in Victoria Park, Bath, at a microcar rally.

An Australian Zeta sports microcar, quite a way from home at a rally near Milton Keynes in Buckinghamshire.

A Lastenroller contemplates a ford near Lower Slaughter in Oxfordshire.

*Parlez vous Francais? A French Inter microcar at Cefartha Castle rally in south Wales.*

*A Frisky in a forest glade near Stanton Drew in Somerset.*

Refuelling a Messerschmitt Tiger in 1963 when the price of petrol was the equivalent of five pence a litre today ...

A rather tatty-looking Nobel pickup and Harper Aloeste at a national microcar rally at Weston Park, Shropshire.

Pretty in pink: a Messerschmitt KR201.

A Goggomobile coupé from Holland visits the Bath microcar rally.

A Reliant 325 keeps company with a Morris lorry of the same period at a rally near Rhode in Somerset.

Above: A Scootacar Mk1 (left) and a Wood Special, complete with stylish paintwork, at a microcar rally near Milton Keynes in Buckinghamshire.

A BSA Ladybird on the cliffs near Eastbourne in Sussex.

A Subaru 360 microcar at Dunkley Beacon on Exmoor in Somerset.

Above: Why carry just a spare wheel? A Peel P50 atop a Range Rover at a national microcar rally at Hatton in Leicestershire.

An early 1950s Reliant Regal coupé pays a visit to the railway workshops at Minehead in west Somerset.

A lovely little Fiat 500 draws much attention at a microcar rally near Milton Keynes in Buckinghamshire.

A Nobel microcar with the River Teign at Shaldon in south Devon as background.

Two-tone Fiat Multipla near the coast at Watermouth Bay in north Devon.

A Frisky four-wheeler at a microcar rally in Weston Park in Shropshire.

A picturesque scene of a Kleinschnittger in the park above Ilfracombe in north Devon.

The name's Bond ... A row of Bond Bugs at a national microcar rally at Hatton in Leicestershire.

# UK club directory

## Scooters

**Lambretta Club of Great Britain**
Kev Walsh
8 Trent Close
Rainhill
Prescot
Merseyside L35 9LD

**Maico Owners Club**
Martin Plummer
Dryad
Jubilee Road
North Somercotes
Louth
Lincs LN11 7LH

**NSU Owners Club**
R Crowley
Nutleigh
Rabies Heath Road
Bletchingly
Surrey RH1 4LX

**Vespa Club Of Great Britain**
Margaret Farquhar
11 Battle Court
Kineton
Warks CV35 0LX

**Veteran Vespa Club**
Peter Rose
28 Greenway
Letchworth
Herts SG6 3UG

**Vintage Motorscooter Club**
Marje Harrop
11 Ivanhoe Avenue
Lowton St
Lukes
Nr Warrington WA3 2HX

**Zundapp Bella Enthusiasts Club**
Bill Dorling
5 Blacklands Road
Upper Bucklebury
Nr Reading
Berkshire

## Microcars

**AC Petite Register**
Alan Budd
5 Bourne Close
Fishbourne
Chichester PO19 3QJ

**Berkeley Enthusiasts**
Peter Hubbard
The Chestnuts
Chequers Road
Tharston
Long Stratton
Norwich NR15 2YA

**Bond Owners Club**
Stan Cornock
42 Beaufort Avenue
Hodge Hill
Birmingham B34 6AE

**Bug Club**
Les Gore
41 Fitchet Close
Langley Green
Crawley
West Sussex

**Fiat 500 Club**
Janet Westcott
33 Lionel Avenue
Wendover
Bucks HP22 6LP

**Fiat 500 and 126 Register**
c/o 118 Brooklands Road
Langport
Somerset TA10 9TM

**Frisky Register**
John Meadows
Graces Cottage

Tregale
Monmouth
Gwent NP5 4RZ

*Goggomobile Register*
Roy Bunker
Fairfields
Horden Dene
Easington
Co Durham SR8 3SS

*Heinkel Trojan Club*
Peter Jones
37 Brinklow Close
Matchborough West
Redditch
Worcs B98 0HB

*Isetta Owners Club*
Kay West
137 Prebendal Avenue
Aylesbury
Bucks HP21 8LD

*Messerschmitt Enthusiasts Club*
Colin Archer
The Old Cottage
Leigh Lane
Wimbourne
Dorset BH21 2PS

*Messerschmitt Owners Club*
Miss Sarah Snowden
8 Russell Court
Chatham
Kent ME4 5LE

*Nobel Register*
Mike Ayriss
29 Oak Drive
Syston
Leicester LE7 2PX

*NSU Owners Club*
Rosie Crowley
Nutleigh
Rabies Heath Road

Bletchingley
Surrey RH11 4LX

*Peel Register*
Steve Hurn
9 Charnwood Drive
Forrest East
Leicester LE3 3HL

*Register of unusual microcars*
Jean Hammond
School House Farm
Boarden Lane
Staplehurst
Kent TN12 0EB

*Reliant Owners Club*
Graham Chappel
19 Smithey Close
High Green
Nr Sheffield S30 4FQ

*Fill 'er up, please! This is the way it used to be: service and personal attention!*

*Scootacar Register*
Stephen Boyd
18 Holman Close
Aylsham
Norwich NR11 6DD

*Trabant UK*
Grayham Goodall
Tor House
Middleton
Bakewell
Derbyshire DE45 1LS

Contact the above national clubs
for details of regional and local
clubs. Also worth a visit are –

*The National Bubblecar Museum*
Byards Leap
Cranwell
Lincolnshire.
NG34 8EY
Tel: 01400 262637

*The National Microcar Museum*
School House Farm
Boarden Lane
Staplehurst
Kent TN12 0EB
Tel: 01580 891377

*The Lambretta Museum*
Weston Scooter Parts
77 Alfred Street
Weston-super-Mare
BS23 1PP
Tel: 01934 614614

Contact the museums in advance
of visiting to ensure volunteer staff
are available to receive and show
you around.

*A Zundapp Bella and period Guy
double decker at a transport rally at
Hengrove in Bristol.*

# Postscript

Thanks must go most of all to the designers and manufacturers of the many scooters and microcars which have given so much pleasure and provided transport convenience to so many people over sixty years of motoring. We also owe a dept of gratitude to those enthusiasts who have invested so much time, money and effort in restoration work which has allowed us to see again these captivating machines from the past; also to those who have, over the years, stored and safeguarded the machines and spares that has made restoration possible. The various owners clubs have also kept the scene alive.

Whilst preparing this book I was asked to specify comparative sales figures for all the different makes and models; an impossible task. It did, however, set me thinking about which were the most popular models in the UK in the fifties and sixties. There are no official figures that I know of to support my views, but I am willing to offer the following as my best estimate of model popularity in the '50s and '60s.

For scooters in the UK, Lambretta must come first, followed by Vespa; unusual, as in virtually every other country Vespa came first. All the others slot in at a very much lower level of sales. I would say the most probable order of the next ten bestsellers in the UK is: Zundapp Bella, Agrati Capri, NSU Prima, BSA Sunbeam/Triumph Tigress, DKR, Puch, Durkopp Diana, Heinkel, Maico, and Dayton. Some makes remained in the market longer, even though annual sales were lower, so had better sales figures overall.

With microcars, for total UK sales first must be Reliant (if you regard these models as microcars, although many people do not!). Otherwise, over the years the most successful must have been Bond, then Isetta, Messerschmitt and Heinkel/Trojan. All of the others come a long way behind.

If anyone can produce statistics to substantiate the foregoing, or prove otherwise, I would be interested to hear. It is curious that some models survived even though sales were low.

Some models, though advertised, were never available in the UK. I remember reading in the relevant magazines about the expected arrival of the British-designed Harper Scootomobile, Bond Sherpa, Renoylds, Pullin Pony and, from Germany, the Venus, from Poland the Osa, and from Czechoslovakia the Hausman, but as far as I know they never appeared on sale in the UK. *Stop press! A 1961 Osa has just surfaced in the UK and is to be restored ...* Others – like the Malanca Vispeta, Victoria Peggy, Aermacchi Harley Davidson, and Monaco – were sold in the UK in very small numbers. They were all interesting designs, and we are the poorer for not seeing them now.

The names of some models changed, like the Jawa Manet scooter which became the Tatran, and the Heinkel bubblecar which became the Trojan. Just as with scooters, some microcars were better known by their model names rather than by their manufacturer; for others the opposite is true.

Sometimes names were changed when production began in another country, as is the case with the Goggo, Nobel and Vespa.

Whenever the subject of scooters from the sixties comes up, it's not long before Mods and Rockers are mentioned. Speaking personally, I began scootering long before the term 'Mod' ever existed, at a time when scooterists were definitely the gentler element of two-wheeled motoring, with no interest at all in the consumption of alcohol or drugs, or shaving their heads! Motorcyclists were the rougher of the two camps, in general considering the scooter – which they referred to as a 'hairdryer' because of its fan cooling and quieter engine noise – a passing phase that wouldn't last (and they were almost proved right!). Despite our obvious differences, however, there was still a lot we had in common even though we didn't realise it at the time. The Mods and their scooters did, at least, look smart and had some style (and kept the accessories market going strong!).

Many scooterists don't appreciate just how big was the range of available scooters; in later years the term 'scooterist' came to denote riders of Vespas or Lambrettas, the only models then available. These two makes had the best sales and stayed in production the longest; they really were the greatest. If I had to choose a winner, though, it would have to be Piaggio with the Vespa, the only model which has stayed in production and is still going strong – in an updated and still very modern form – today. That's pretty good for a machine originally considered to be based on an unstable design!

Piaggio really hit the nail on the head with the Vespa, the first scooter to offer stylish, economic

*A Vespa Cosa on the beach at Beer in south Devon.*

personal transport at a third of the cost of a car. It was easy to sit on and ride, and had an easily fitted spare wheel. All of its mechanics were covered up, protecting the rider from oil and dirt. Refreshing and new when life after the Second World War was rather grim and dull, the Vespa appealed to both sexes and sold in very large numbers for over twenty years, enjoying worldwide popularity. It became a legend in its home country and played a large part in the regeneration of Italy after the war.

In the world of microcars the UK winner must be Laurie Bond and his Minicar. Bond's microcar designs were also taken up by other companies such as Opperman and Berkeley, and even today there is a modern microcar importer which trades under the name of Bond.

On the continent Piaggio – with its French-made Vespa 400 microcar – was poised for large sales before being forced to end production when Fiat – manufacturer of 500 and 600cc cars – said that unless Piaggio forgot about small car production, it would begin scooter manufacture! In Germany, Glas – with the Goggomobile – sold more microcars than anyone else.

The rise and fall and rise again of the scooter and, to a lesser extent, the microcar, has been very symbolic of the turbulence experienced in the motor industry in general. When microcars first appeared in the UK many great British companies were making motorcycles; household names of the time such as Ambassador, Ariel, Sun, BSA, Triumph, DMW, Excelsior, Panther, Douglas, Velocette, and James, all of which later went on to make scooters. AJS, Norton, Greeves, Norman, Dot, Scott, Sunbeam, Matchless, Royal Enfield, Francis Barnet, Rudge, and Cotton didn't, and soon went out of business. (All of the companies I've mentioned closed down within the next twenty years in any case.) Hard to comprehend, even when it happened: the end of a great industry.

Today, enthusiast clubs and magazines encourage participation in the restoration scene, which can be great fun and a way to meet many interesting and like-minded people. For more information on this aspect please contact the club addresses given in the club directory, or buy the current copy of *Scootering Magazine* which not only deals with modern machines but regularly features the classics, too.

It has been estimated that, since the original

The author's Smart Passion, complete with personalised number plate, in the hills near Nether Stowey in west Somerset.

scooter boom years of the 1950s, over a million people in Britain have had an association with scooters and microcars. I have not been fortunate enough to keep all of my restorations, much as I would like to have done, but do still have, however, a recreation of the first vehicle I ever owned, which began my obsession! I have fond memories of all of the many makes and models which the photographs in this book go a long way toward preserving.

Thank you for buying my book; I hope you enjoyed reading it as much as I enjoyed preparing the material, at the same time reliving all of the happy memories it brought flooding back ...

## Dedication

Remembering Jim Parkinson, a true enthusiast. In 1965, Jim rode a 1935 Rytecraft Scootacar with a tiny Villiers engine across the USA, Europe and Japan. In later years, a visit to his bookstall at classic shows was always a rewarding experience.

# Famous 1950s and 1960s scooter and microcar importers

BP Scooters, Wolverhampton
International Sales Ltd, London
Rhyders Autoservice, Liverpool
Douglas Ltd, Bristol
Nannucci Ltd, London
Ambassador Motorcycles Ltd, Ascot
Isetta of Great Britain, Brighton
Scooter Concessionaires Ltd, London
Bolton Motorcyles Ltd
NSU Great Britain, London
Stuart and Payne, London
Lambretta Concessionaires, London
Industria, London
Scooter and Vehicles Concessionaires Ltd, London
International Sales Ltd, London

Progress Supreme Co, Purley
Cabin Scooters (Assemblies) Ltd, London
Europa Imports, Reading
Robert Eden and Co, London
Diana Concessionaires, Ruislip
AFN Ltd, Isleworth
Maico Great Britain Ltd, London
Phelon and Moore, Cleckheaton
Motor Imports Ltd
Hans Motors, London
Nobel Motors Ltd, London
Capri Scooters Ltd, Nottingham
R and C Autocars, London
FH Warr Ltd, London
York Noble Industries Ltd, London

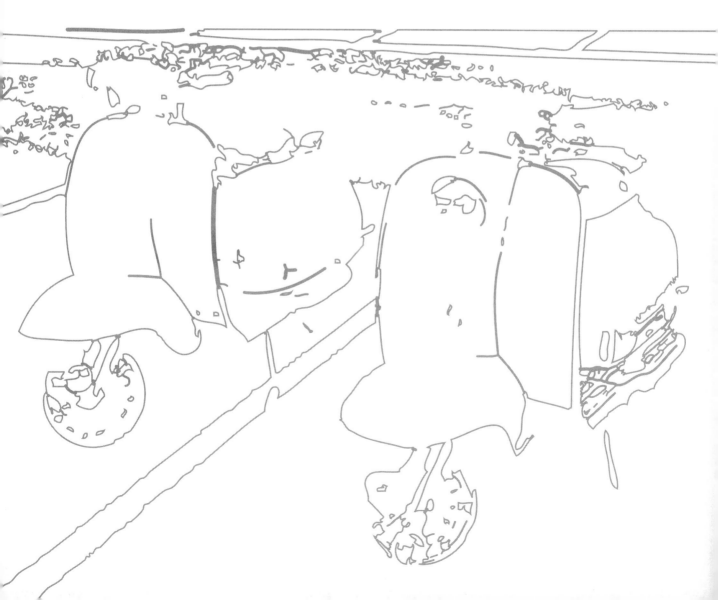

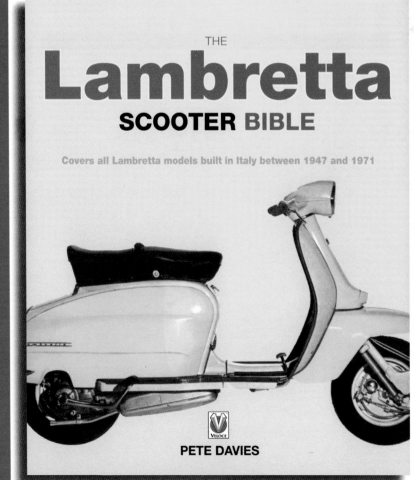

Adam Quellin

# MICROCARS AT LARGE!

VELOCE

The history and development – with original colour photographs – of the small economy cars that emerged after the Second World War. Bubblecars, as they became affectionately known, provided transport for thousands of impoverished motorists during that lean period, and now these tiny economy cars have a significant place in motoring history.

£14.99•112 pages•113 colour photographs
paperback•ISBN: 9781845840921

# Index

Fiat is perhaps best known for its ability to produce small, economical, characterful cars. This book traces that concept from the birth of the 500A 'Topolino' in the 1930s up to the current Panda and a hint of the proposed Nuova 500. Each of the selected models is described in detail from conception through to current ownership in the hands of collectors and enthusiasts.

£16.99 • 176 pages • 200 illustrations
• paperback • ISBN: 9781845841331

p&p extra; please call 01305 260068 for rates or visit www.veloce.co.uk

# Great Small FIATs

FIAT ABARTH 595

VELOCE

**Phil Ward**